The Nature of Human Brain Work

Joseph Dietzgen

AAKAR

THE NATURE OF HUMAN BRAIN WORK
Joseph Dietzgen

Published in agreement with PM Press, Oakland, CA
for publication and sale only in the Indian Subcontinent
(India, Pakistan, Bangladesh, Nepal, Maldives,
Bhutan & Sri Lanka)

First Published in India, 2011

ISBN 978-93-5002-053-1 (Pb)

Published by
AAKAR BOOKS
28 E Pocket IV, Mayur Vihar Phase I, Delhi 110 091
Phone : 011 2279 5505 Telefax : 011 2279 5641
aakarbooks@gmail.com; www.aakarbooks.com

Printed at
Mudrak, 30 A, Patparganj, Delhi 110 091

Contents

I
Introduction

Systematization is the essence and the general expression of the aggregate activity of science. Science seeks to classify and systematize the objects of the world for the understanding of our brain. The scientific understanding of a certain language, e.g., requires an orderly arrangement of that language in general categories and rules. The science of agriculture does not simply wish to produce a good crop of potatoes, but to find a system for the methods of cultivation and thus to furnish the knowledge by which success in cultivation can be determined beforehand. The practical result of all theory is to acquaint us with the system and method of its practice and thus to enable us to act in this world with a reasonable certainty of success. Experience is, of course, an indispensable condition for this purpose; but it alone is not sufficient. Only by means of empirically developed theories; by science, do we overcome the play of accident. Science gives us the conscious domination over things and unconditional security in handling them.

No one individual can know everything. The capacity of the individual brain is no more adequate for the knowledge of everything that is necessary than the skill and strength of the individual's hands are sufficient to produce all he needs. Faith is indispensable to man, but only faith in that which others know, not in what they believe. Science is as much a social matter as material production. "One for all and all for one."

But just as there are some wants of the body which every one has to satisfy by himself, so every one has to know certain scientific facts which are not the prerogative of any special science. This is true of the faculty of human understanding. The knowledge and study of this theory cannot be left to any particular guild. Lassalle justly says, "Thinking itself has become a special trade in these days of division of labor, and it has fallen into the worst hands, those of our newspaper writers." He thus urges us not to acquiesce in this appropriation any longer, not to submit any more to the harangues of public opinion, but to resume thinking for ourselves, we may leave certain objects of scientific research to professionals, but general thought is a public matter which every one should be required to attend to himself.

If we could place this general work of thinking on a scientific basis, if we could find a theory of general thought, if we were able to discover the means by which reason arrives at understanding, if we could develop a method by which truth is produced scientifically, then we should acquire for science, in general and for our individual faculty of judgment the same certainty of success which we already possess in special fields of science.

Kant says, "If it is not possible to harmonize the various cooperators on the question of the means by which their common aim is to be accomplished, then we may safely infer that such a study is not yet on the secure road of science, but will continue to grope in the dark."

Now, if we take a look at the sciences, we find that there are many, especially among the natural sciences, which fulfill the requirements of Kant, agreeing unanimously and consciously on certain empirical knowledge and building further understanding on that. "There we know," as Liebig says, "what is to be called a certain fact, a conclusion, a rule, a law. We have touchstones for all this, and every one makes use of them before making known the fruits of his labors. The attempt to maintain any proposition by lawyer's tricks, or the intention to make others believe anything that cannot be proven, are immediately wrecked by the ethics of science."

Not so in other fields, where concrete and material things are left behind and abstract, so-called philosophical, matters are taken up, as, for instance, questions of general conceptions of the world and of life, of beginning and end, of the semblance and the essence of things, of cause and effect, of matter and force, of might and right, of wisdom of life, of morality, religion, and politics. Here we find, instead of irrefutable proofs, mere "lawyer's tricks," an absence of reliable knowledge, a mere groping amid contradictory opinions.

And it is precisely the prominent authorities of natural science who show by their disagreements on such matters that they are mere tyros in philosophy. It follows, then, that the so-called ethics of science, the touchstones of which the boast is made that they never fail in determining what is knowledge and what is mere conjecture, are based on a purely instinctive practice, not on a conscious theory of understanding. Although our time excels in diligent scientific research, yet the numerous differences among scientists show that they are not capable of using their knowledge with a predetermined certainty of success. Otherwise, how could misunderstandings arise? Whoever understands understanding, cannot misunderstand. It is only the absolute accuracy of astronomical computations which entitles astronomy to the name of a science. A man who can figure is at least enabled to test whether his computation is right or wrong. In the same way, the general understanding of the process of thought must furnish us with the touchstone by which we can distinguish between understanding and misunderstanding, knowledge and conjecture, truth and error, by general and irrefutable rules. Erring is human, but not scientific. Science being a human matter, errors may exist eternally, but the understanding of the process of thought will enable us quite as well to prevent errors from being offered and accepted as scientific truths as an understanding of mathematics enables us to eliminate errors from our computations.

It sounds paradoxical and yet it is true: Whoever knows the general rule by which error may be distinguished from truth, and knows it as well as the rule in grammar by which a noun is distinguished from a verb, will be able to distinguish in both cases with equal certainty. Scientists as well as scribes have ever embarrassed one another by the question: What is truth? This question has been an essential object of philosophy for thousands of years. This question, like philosophy itself, is finally settled by the understanding of the faculty of human thought. In other words, the question of what constitutes truth is identical with the question of the distinction between truth and error. Philosophy is the science which has been engaged in solving this riddle, and the final solution of the riddle by the clear understanding of the process of thought also solves the question of the nature of philosophy. Hence a short glance at the nature and development of philosophy may well serve as an introduction to our study.

As the word philosophy is connected with various meanings, I state at the outset that I am referring only to so-called speculative philosophy. I dispense with frequent quotations and notes of the sources of my knowleage, as anything that I may say in this respect is so well established that we can afford to discard all scientific by-work.

If we apply the above-named test of Kant to speculative philosophy it appears to be more the playground of different opinions than of science. The philosophical celebrities and classic authorities are not even in accord on the question: what is philosophy and what is its aim? For this reason, and in order not to increase the difference by adding my own opinion, I regard everything as philosophy that calls itself by that name, and we select from the voluminous literature of philosophy that which is common and general in all philosophers, without taking any notice of their special peculiarities.

By this empirical method we find first of all that philosophy is originally not a specialized science working with other sciences, but a generic name for all knowledge, the essence of all science, just as art is the essence of the various arts. Whoever made knowledge, whoever made brain work his essential occupation, every thinker without regard to the contents of his thoughts, was originally a philosopher.

But when with the progressive increase of human knowledge, the various departments detached themselves from the mother of all wisdom, especially since the origin of natural sciences, philosophy became known, not so much by its content as by its form. All other sciences are distinguished by their various objects, while philosophy is marked by its own method. Of course, it also has its object and purpose it desires to understand the universal whole, the cosmos. But it is not this object, this aim, by which philosophy is characterized; It is rather the manner in which this object is accomplished.

All other sciences occupy themselves with special things, and if they consider the universe at all, they do so only in its bearing on the special objects of their study, the parts of which the universe is composed. Alexander von Humboldt says in his introduction to his "Cosmos" that he is limiting himself to an empirical consideration, to a physical research, which seeks to elucidate the uniformity and unity by means of the great variety. And all inductive sciences arrive at general conclusions and conceptions only by way of their occupation with special and concrete things.

For this reason they claim that their conclusions are based on facts.

Speculative philosophy proceeds by the opposite method. Thought, the object of its study, may be some special question, yet it does not follow this up in the concrete. It rejects as fallacious the evidence of the senses, the physical experience gained by means of the eye and ear, hand and brain, and limits itself to "pure" and absolutely abstract thought, in order to understand thus by the unit of human reason the multiplicity of the universe. In seeking for an answer to the question: What is philosophy? which question we are specially discussing, just now, speculative philosophy would not start out from its actual material form, from its wooden and pigskin volumes, from its great and small essays, in order to arrive at a conception of its object. On the contrary, the speculative philosopher turns to introspection and looks in the depths of his own mind for the true concept of philosophy. And by this standard he separates the impression of his senses into true or erroneous. This speculative method has hardly ever dealt in tangible things, unless we recognize this philosophical method in every unscientific concept of nature which populated the world with spooks. The rudiments of scientific speculation occasionally dealt with the course of the sun and the globe. But since inductive astronomy cultivates these fields with greater success, speculative philosophy limits itself entirely to abstract discussions. And in this line of research as well as in all others it is characterized by the production of its results out of the idea or the concept.

For empirical science, for the inductive method, the multiplicity of experiences is the first basis, and thought the second. Speculative philosophy, on the other hand, seeks to arrive at scientific truth without the help of experience. It rejects the so-called transient facts as a foundation of philosophical understanding, and declares that it should be absolute, exalted above time and space. Speculative philosophy does not wish to be scientific physics, but metaphysics. It regards it as its task to find by "pure" reason, and without the assistance of experience, a system, a logic, or a theory of science, by which everything worth knowing is supposed to be reeled off logically and systematically, in about the same way in which we derive grammatically the various forms of a word from its root. But the physical sciences operate on the assumption that our faculty of understanding, to use a familiar illustration, resembles a piece of soft wax which receives impressions from outside, or a clean slate on which experience writes its lines. Speculative philosophy, on the other hand, assumes that certain ideas are innate and may be dipped and produced from the depths of the mind by means of thought.

The difference between speculative and inductive science is that between fantasy and sound common sense. The latter produces its ideas by means of the outer world, by the help of experience, while fantasy gets its product from the depth of the mind, out of itself.

But this method of production is only seemingly one-sided. A thinker can no more think transcendental thoughts which are beyond the reach of experience, than a painter can invent transcendental pictures, transcendental forms. Just as fantasy creates angels by a combination of man and bird, or mermaids by a composition of woman and fish, while other products of fantasy, though seemingly derived out of itself, are in fact only arbitrarily arranged impressions of the outer world. Reason operates with numbers and orders, time and measures, and other means of experience, while fantasy reproduces the experiences without regard to law and in an arbitrary form.

The longing for knowledge has been the cause of speculative attempts to explain the phenomena of life and nature at a time when lack of experience and observation made inductive understanding impossible. Experience was then supplemented by speculation. In later times, when experience had grown, previous speculation was generally recognized as erroneous. But it nevertheless required thousands of years of repeated disappointments on one side and numerous brilliant successes of the inductive method on the other, before these speculative hobbies came into disfavor.

Fantasy has certainly a positive power, and speculative intuition, derived from analogy, very often precedes empirical and inductive understanding. But we must remain aware of the fact that so much is assumption and so much actual scientific knowledge. Conscious intuition stimulates scientific research, while pseudo-science closes the door to inductive research. The acquisition of the clear understanding of the distinction between speculation and knowledge is a historical process, the beginning and end of which coincides with the beginning and end of speculative philosophy.

In ancient times, common sense operated in common with fantasy, the inductive within the speculative method. The discussion of their differences begins only with the understanding of the numerous disappointments caused by the still inexperienced judgment which have prevented an unobstructed view of the question up to modern times. But instead of attributing these disappointments to lack of understanding, they were charged to the account of the imperfection of the senses. The senses were called impostors and material phenomena untrue images. Who has not heard the lament about the unreliability of the senses? The misunderstanding of nature and of its phenomena led to a serious rupture with sense perceptions. The philosophers had deceived themselves and thought they had been deceived by the senses. In their anger they turned disdainfully away from the world of sensations. With the same uncritical faith with which the semblance had hitherto been accepted as truth, now uncritical doubt rejected the truth of sensations altogether. Research abandoned nature and experience, and began the work of speculative philosophy by "pure" thought.

But no! Science did not permit itself to be entirely led astray from the path of common sense, from the way of truth of sense perceptions. Natural science soon stepped into the breach, and its brilliant successes gained for the inductive method the consciousness of its fertility, while on the other hand philosophy searched for a system by which all the great general truths might be opened up without specialized study, without sense perception and observation, by mere reason alone.

Now we have a more than sufficient quantity of such speculative systems. If we measure them with the aforementioned standard of unanimousness, we find that philosophy agrees only on its disagreements. In consequence, the history of speculative philosophy, unlike the history of other sciences, consists less of a gradual accumulation of knowledge, than of a series of unsuccessful attempts to solve the general riddles of nature and life by "pure" thought, without the help of the objects and experience of the outer world. The most daring attempt in this line, the most artificial structure of thought, was completed by Hegel in the beginning of the nineteenth century. To use a common expression, he became as famous in the world of science as Napoleon I did in the world of politics. But, Hegelian philosophy has not stood the test of time. Haym, in his work entitled "Hegel and His Time," says of Hegelian philosophy that "it was pushed aside by the progress of the world and by living history."

The outcome of philosophy up to that time, then, was a declaration of its own impotence. Nevertheless, we do not underestimate the fact that a work occupying the best brains for thousands of years surely contained some positive element. And in fact, speculative philosophy has a history, which is not merely a series of unsuccessful attempts, but also a living development. However, it is less the object of its study, less the logical world system, which developed, than its method.

Every positive science has a material object, a beginning in the outer world, a premise on which its understanding is based. Every empirical science has for its fundament some material of the senses, some given object, on which its understanding is dependent, and thus it becomes "impure." Speculative philosophy seeks a "pure, absolute," understanding. It wishes to understand by "pure" reason, without any material, without any experience. It takes its departure from the enthusiastic conviction of the superiority of understanding and knowledge over experience gained by sense perceptions. For this reason it wishes to leave experience entirely aside in favor the absolutely "pure" understanding. Its object is truth not concrete truth, not the truth of this or that thing; but truth in general, truth "in itself." The speculative systems seek after an absolute beginning, an indubitably self-supporting starting point, from which they may determine the absolutely indubitable. The speculative systems are thus by their own mentality perfectly complete and self-sufficient systems. Every speculative system found its end in the subsequent knowledge that its totality, its self-sufficiency, its absoluteness, was imaginary, that it could be determined empirically and externally like all other knowledge, that it was not a philosophical system, but a relative and empirical attempt at understanding. Speculation finally dissolved into the knowledge that understanding is by its very nature "impure," that the organ of philosophy, the faculty of understanding cannot begin its studies without a given point of departure, that science is not absolutely superior to experience, but only so far as it can organize numerous experiences. It followed from these premises that the object of philosophy can be a general and objective understanding, or "truth in itself," only in so far as understanding or truth in general can be derived from given concrete objects. In plain word speculative philosophy was reduced to the unphilosophical science of the empirical faculty of understanding, to the critique of reason.

Modern conscious speculation takes its departure from the experienced difference between semblance and truth. It denies all sense phenomena in order to find truth by thinking, without being deceived by any semblance. The subsequent philosophers, however, found every time that the truths of their predecessors, gained by this method, were not what they pretended to be, but that their positive result consisted simply in having advanced the science of the thought process to a certain extent. By denying the actuality of the senses, by endeavoring to separate thought from all sense perceptions, by isolating it, so to say, from its sensory cover, speculative philosophy, more than any other science, laid bare the structure of the mind. The more this philosophy advanced in time, the more it developed in its historical course, the more classically and strikingly did this kernel of its work spring into view. After the repeated creation of giant fantasmagorias, it found its solution in the positive knowledge that so-called pure philosophical thought, abstracting from all concrete contents, is nothing but thoughtless thought, thought without any real object back of it, and produces mere fantasmagorias. This process of speculative deception and scientific exposure was continued up to recent times. Finally the solution of the main question, and the solution of speculation, was introduced with the following words of Feuerbach: "My philosophy is no philosophy."

The long story of speculative work was finally reduced to the understanding of reason, of the intellect, the mind, to the exposure of those mysterious operations which we call thinking.

The secret of the processes by which the truths of understanding are produced, the ignorance of the fact that every thought requires an object, a premise, was the cause of the idle speculative wanderings which we find registered in the history of philosophy. The same secret is today the cause of those numerous speculative mistakes which we observe in passing over the words and works of naturalists. Their knowledge and understanding is far developed, but only so far as it refers to tangible objects. The moment they touch upon abstract discussions, they offer "lawyers' proofs" in place of "objective facts." For although they know intuitively and in a concrete case that this is a truth, that a conclusion, and that a rule, they do not apply this knowledge in general with consciousness and theoretical consistency. The successes of natural science have taught them to operate the instrument of thought, the mind, instinctively. But they lack the systematic understanding which operates with conscious and predetermined certainty. They ignore the outcome of speculative philosophy.

It will be our task to set forth in a short summary what speculative philosophy has unconsciously produced of a positive nature by a tedious process, in other words, to explain the general nature of the thought process. We shall see that the understanding of this process will furnish us with the means of solving scientifically the general riddles of nature and of life. And thus we shall learn how that fundamental and systematic world conception is developed which was the long coveted goal of speculative philosophy.

II

Pure Reason or the Faculty of Thought in General

When speaking of food in general, we may mention fruits, cereals, vegetables, meat and bread and classify them all, in spite of their difference, under this one head. In the same way, we use, in this work, the terms reason, consciousness, intellect, knowledge, discernment, understanding, as referring to the same general thing. For we are discussing the general nature of the thought process rather than its special forms.

"No intelligent thinker of our day," says a modern physiologist, "pretends to look for the seat of the intellectual powers in the blood, as did the ancient Greeks, or in the pineal gland, as was the case in the middle ages. Instead we have all become convinced that the central nerve system is the organic center of the intellectual functions of the brain." Yes, true enough, thinking is a function of the brain and nerve centre, just as writing is a function of the hand. But the study of the anatomy of the hand can no more solve the question: What is writing? than the physiological study of the brain can bring us nearer to the solution of the question: What is thought? With the dissecting knife, we may kill, but we cannot discover the mind. The understanding that thought is a product of the brain takes us closer to the solution of our problem, in as much as it draws it into the bright light of reality and out of the domain of fantasy in which the ghosts dwell. Mind thereby loses the character of a transcendental incomprehensible being and appears as a bodily function.

Thinking is a function of the brain just as walking is a function of the legs. We perceive thought and mind just as clearly with our senses as we do pain and other feelings. Thought is felt by us as a subjective process taking place inside of us. According to its contents this process varies every moment and with each person, but according to its form it is the same everywhere. In other words, in the thought process, as in all processes, we make a distinction between the special or concrete and the general or abstract. The general purpose of thought is understanding. We shall see later that the simplest conception, or any idea for that matter, is of the same general nature as the most perfect understanding.

Thought and understanding cannot be without subjective contents any more than without an object which suggests individual reflection. Thought is work, and like every other work it requires an object to which it is applied. The statements: I do, I work, I think, must be completed by an answer to the question; What are you doing, working, thinking?

Every definite idea, all actual thought, is identical with its content, but not with its object. My desk as a picture in my mind is identical with my idea of it. But my desk outside of my brain is a separate object and distinct from my idea. The idea is to be distinguished from thinking only as a part of the thought process, while the object of my thought exists as a separate entity.

We make a distinction between thinking and being. We distinguish between the object of sense perception and its mental image. Nevertheless the intangible idea is also material and real. I perceive my idea of a desk just as plainly as the desk itself. True, if I choose to call only tangible things material, then ideas are not material. But in that case the scent of a rose and the heat of a stove are not material. It would be better to call thoughts sense perceptions. But if it is objected that this would be an incorrect use of the word, because language distinguishes material and mental things, then we dispense with the word material and call thought real. Mind is as real as the tangible table, as the visible light, as the audible sound. While the idea of these things is different from the things themselves, yet it has that in common with them that it is as real as they. Mind is not any more different from a table, a light, a sound, than these things differ among themselves. We do not deny that there is a difference. We merely emphasize that they have the same general nature in common. I hope the reader will not misunderstand me henceforth, when I call the faculty of thought a material quality, a phenomenon of sense perception.

Every perception of the senses is based on some object. In order that heat may be real, there must be an object, something else which is heated. The active cannot exist without the passive. The visible cannot exist without the faculty of sight, nor the faculty of sight without visible things. So is the faculty of thought a phenomenon, but it can never exist in itself, it must always be based on some sense perception. Thought appears, like all other phenomena, in connection with an object. The function of the brain is no more a "pure" process than the function of the eye, the scent of a flower, the heat of a stove, or the touch of a table. The fact that a table may be seen, heard, or felt, is due as much to its own nature as to that of another object with which it enters into some relation.

But while each function is limited by its own separate line of objects, while the function of the eye serves only for the perception of the visible, the hand for the tangible, while walking finds an object in the space it crosses, thought, on the other hand, has everything for its object.

Everything may be the object of understanding. Thought is not limited to any special object. Every phenomenon may be the object and the content of thought. More than this, we can only perceive anything when it becomes the object of our brain activity. Everything is therefore the object and content of thought. The faculty of thought may be exerted quite generally on all objects.

We said a moment ago that everything may be perceived, but we now modify this to the effect that only perceivable things may be perceived. Only the knowable can be the object of knowledge, only the thinkable the object of thought. To this extent the faculty of thought is limited, for it cannot replace reading, hearing, feeling, and all other innumerable activities of the world of sensations. We do, indeed, perceive all objects, but no object may be exhaustively perceived, known, or understood. In other words, the objects are not wholly dissolved in the understanding. Seeing requires something that is visible, something which is, therefore, more than seeing. In the same way, hearing requires something that can be heard, thinking an object that can be thought of, something which is more than our thoughts, something still outside of our consciousness. We shall learn later on how we arrive at the knowledge that we see, hear, feel, and think of objects, and not merely of subjective impressions.

By means of thought we become aware of all things in a twofold manner, viz., outside in reality and inside in thought, in conception. It is easy to demonstrate that the things outside are different from the things in our thoughts. In their actual form, in their real dimensions, they cannot enter into our heads. Our brain does not assimilate the things themselves, but only their images, their general outlines. The imagined tree is only a general object. The real tree is different from any other. And though I may have a picture of some special tree in my head, yet the real tree is still as different from its conception as the special is different from the general. The infinite variety of things, the innumerable wealth of their properties, has no room in our heads.

I repeat, then, that we become aware of the outer world in a twofold way, viz., in a concrete, tangible, manifold form, and in an abstract form, which is mental and unitary. To our senses the world appears as a variety of forms. Our brains combine them as a unit. And what is true of the world, holds good of every one of its parts. A sense-perceived unit is a nonentity. Even the atom of a drop of water or the atom of any chemical element, is divisible, so long as it exists at all, and its parts are different and distinct. A is not B. But the concept, the faculty of thought, makes of every tangible or sense-perceived part an abstract whole and conceives of every whole or quantity as a part of the abstract world unit. In order to understand the things in their entirety, we must take them practically and theoretically, with body and mind. With the body we can grasp only the bodily, the tangible, with the mind only the mental, the thinkable. Things also possess mental quality. Mind is material and things are mental. Mind and matter are real only in their inter-relations.

Can we see the things themselves? No, we see only the effects of things on our eyes. We do not taste the vinegar, but the relation of the vinegar to our tongue. The result is the sensation of acidity. The vinegar is acid only in relation to our tongue. In relation to iron it acts as a solvent. In the cold it becomes hard, in the heat liquid. It acts differently on different objects with which it enters into relations of time and space. Vinegar is a phenomenon, just as all things are. But it never appears as vinegar by itself. It always appears in connection with other phenomena. Every phenomenon is a product of a subject and an object.

In order that a thought may appear, the brain or the faculty of thought is not sufficient in itself. It requires, besides, an object which suggests the thought. From this relative nature of our topic it follows that in its treatment we cannot confine ourselves "purely" to it. Since reason, or the faculty of thought, never appears by itself, but always in connection with other things, we are continually compelled to pass from the the faculty of thought to other things, which are its objects, and to treat of their connections.

Just as the sight does not see the tree, but only that which is visible of the tree, so does the faculty of thought assimilate only the perceivable image of an object, not the object itself. A thought is a child begotten by the function of the brain in communion with some object. In a thought is crystallized on one side the subjective faculty of thought, and on the other the perceivable nature of an object. Every function of the mind presupposes some object by which it is caused and the spiritual image of which it is. Or vice versa, the spiritual content of the mind is derived from some object which has its own existence and which is either seen or heard, or smelled, or tasted, or felt, in short, experienced.

Referring back to the statement that seeing is limited to the visible qualities of some object, hearing to its audible qualities, etc., while the faculty of thought has everything for its object, we now understand this to mean that all objects have certain innumerable, but concrete, qualities which are perceptible by our senses, and in addition thereto the general spiritual quality of being thought of, understood, in short, of being the object of our faculty of thought.

This mode of classifying all objects applies also to the faculty of thought itself. The spirit, or mind, is a bodily function connected with the senses which appear in various forms. Mind is thought generated at different times in different brains by different objects through the instrumentality of the senses, we may choose this mind as the object of special thought the same as all other things. Considered as an object, mind is a many-sided and sense-perceived fact which in connection with a special function of the brain generates the general concept of "Mind" as the content of this special thought process. The object of thought is distinguished from its contents in the same way in which every object is distinguished from its mental image. The different kinds of motion perceived by the help of the senses are the object of a certain thought process and supply to it the idea of "motion." It is easier to understand that the mental image of some object perceived by the senses has a father and a mother, being begotten by our faculty of thought by means of some sense-perceived object, than it is to grasp the existence of that trinity which is born when our present thought experiences its own existence and thus creates a conception of its own self. This has the appearance of moving around in a circle. The object, the content and the function of thought apparently coincide. Reason deals with itself, considers itself as an object and is its own content. But nevertheless the distinction between an object and its concept, though less evident, is just as actual as in other cases. It is only the habit of regarding matter and mind as fundamentally different things which conceals this truth. The necessity to make a distinction compels us everywhere to discriminate between the object of sense perception and its mental concept. We are forced to do the same in the case of the faculty of thought, and thus we find it necessary to give the name of "Mind" to this special object of our sense perceptions. Such an ambiguity of terms cannot be entirely avoided in any science. A reader who does not cling to words, but rather seeks to grasp the meaning will easily realize that the difference between being and thinking applies also to the faculty of thought, that the fact of understanding is different from the understanding of understanding. And since the understanding of understanding is again another fact, it will be permitted to call all spiritual things facts or sense perceptions.

Reason, or the faculty of thought, is therefore not a mystical object which produces the individual thought. On the contrary, it is a fact that certain individual thoughts are the product of perception gained in contact with certain objects and that these in connection with a certain brain operation produce the concept of reason. Reason as well as all other things of which we became aware has a two-fold existence one as a phenomenon or sense-perception, the other as a concept. The concept of any thing presupposes a certain sense-perception of that thing, and so does the concept of reason. Since all men think as a matter of fact, every one has himself perceived reason as a part of reality, as a phenomenon, sense perception or fact.

Our object, reason, by virtue of the fact that it partakes of the nature of the senses, has the faculty of transforming the speculative method, which tries to dip understanding out of the depths of the spirit without the help of sense-perception, into the inductive method, and vice versa of transforming the inductive method, which desires to arrive at conclusions, concepts, or understanding exclusively by means of sense perception, into the speculative method, by virtue of its simultaneous spiritual nature. Our problem is to analyze the concept of thought, or of the faculty of thought, or of reason, of knowing, of science, by means of thought.

To produce thoughts and to analyze them is the same thing inasmuch as both actions are functions of the brain. Both have the same nature. But they are different to the same extent that instinct differs from consciousness. Man does not think originally because he wants to, but because he must. Ideas are produced instinctively, involuntarily. In order to become fully aware of them, to place them within the grasp all-knowing and willing, we must analyze them. From the experience of walking, for instance, we derive the: idea of walking. To analyze this idea means to solve the question, what is walking generally considered what is the general nature of walking?' We may answer: Walking is a rhythmical motion from one place to another, and thus we raise the instinctive idea to the position of a conscious analyzed idea. An object is not consciously, theoretically, understood, until it has been analyzed. In examining what elements constitute the concept of walking, we find that the general attribute of that experience which we agree in calling "walking" is a rhythmical motion. In actual experience steps may be long or short, may be taken by two feet or by more, in brief may be varied. But as a concept walking is simply a rhythmical motion, and the analysis of this concept furnishes us with the conscious understanding of this fact. The concept of light existed long before science analyzed it, before it was understood that undulations of the ether form the elements which constitute the concept of light. Instinctive and analytical ideas differ in the same way in which the thoughts of every day life differ from the thoughts of science.

The analysis of any idea and the theoretical analysis of any object, or of the thing which suggested the idea, is one and the same. Every idea corresponds to some real object. Ludwig Feuerbach has demonstrated that even the concepts of God and immortality are reflections of real objects which can be perceived by the senses. For the purpose of analyzing such ideas as animal, light, friendship, man, etc., the phenomena, the objects, such as animals, friendships, men, and lights, are analyzed. The object which selves for the analysis of the concept "animal" is no more any single animal, than the object of the concept "light" is any single light.

These concepts comprise classes, things in general, and therefore the question, or the analysis, of what constitutes the animal, the light, friendship, must not deal with any concrete, but with the abstract elements of the whole class.

The fact that the analysis of a concept and the analysis of its object appear as two different things is due to our faculty of being able to separate things into two parts, viz., into a practical, tangible, perceptible, concrete thing and into a theoretical mental, thinkable, general thing. The practical analysis is the premise of the theoretical analysis. The individually perceptible animals serve us as a basis for the analysis of the animal concept, the individually experienced friendships as the basis for the analysis of the concept of friendship.

Every idea corresponds to an object which may be practically separated into its component parts. To analyze a concept is equivalent, therefore, to analyzing a previously experienced object by theoretical means. The analysis of a concept consists in the understanding of the common or general faculties of the concrete parts of the analyzed object. That which is common to the various modes of walking, the rhythmical motion, constitutes the concept of walking, that which is common to the various manifestations of light constitutes the concept of light. A chemical factory analyzes objects for the purpose of obtaining chemicals, while science analyzes them for the purpose of obtaining their concepts.

The special object of our analysis, the faculty of thought, is likewise distinguished from its concept. But in order to be able to analyze this concept, we must analyze the object. It cannot be analyzed chemically, for not everything is a matter of chemistry, but it may be analyzed theoretically or scientifically. As we have already stated, the science of understanding deals with all objects. But all objects which this science may wish to analyze theoretically, must first be handled practically. According to their special natures, they must either be handled in various ways, or carefully inspected; or scrutinized by intent listening, in short they must be thoroughly experienced in some way.

It is a fact of experience that men think. The object or suggestion is furnished by facts, and we then derive the concept instinctively. Thus, to analyze the faculty of thought means to find that which is common or general to the various personal and temporary processes of thought. In order to follow this study by the methods of natural science, we require neither physical instruments nor chemical reagents. The sense perception which is indispensable for every scientific understanding, is so to say present in this case *a priori*, without further experience. Every one possesses the object of our study, the fact of thought faculty and its experience, in the memories of himself or herself.

We have seen that thought like any other activity as well as its scientific analysis is everywhere developing the general or abstract out of particular and concrete sense perceptions. We now express this in the following words: The common feature of all separate thought-processes consists in their seeking the general character or unity which is common to all objects experienced in their manifold variety by sense perceptions. The general element which is common to the different animals, or to the different manifestations of light, is that which constitutes the general animal or light concept. The general is the nature of all concepts, of all understanding, all science, all thought processes. Thus we arrive at the understanding that the analysis of the faculty of thought reveals its nature of finding that which is general and common to concrete and distinct things. The eye studies the visible, the ear the audible, and our brain that which is generally conceivable.

We have seen that thought like any other activity requires an object; that it is unlimited in the choice of its objects, because all things may become the objects of thought; that these objects are perceived in manifold forms by various senses; and that they are transformed into simple ideas by extricating that which they possess in common, which is similar, which is general in them. If we apply this experience experienced understanding of the general method of thought processes to our special object, the faculty of thought, we realize that we have thus solved our problem, because all we were looking for was the general method of the thought process.

If the development of the general out of the concrete constitutes the general method by which reason arrives at understanding, then we have fully grasped reason as the faculty of deriving the general out of the concrete.

Thinking is a physical process and it cannot exist or produce anything without materials any more than any other process of labor. My thought requires some material which can be thought of. This material is furnished by the phenomena of nature and life. These are the concrete things. In claiming that the universe, or all things, may be the object of thought, we simply mean that the materials of the thought process, the objects of the mind, are infinite in quantity and quality. The materials which the universe furnishes for our thought are as infinite as space, as eternal as time, and as absolutely manifold as the nature of these two forms of being. The faculty of thought is a universal faculty in so far as it enters into relations with all things, all substances, all phenomena, and thus generates thought. But it is not absolute, since it requires for its existence and action the previous presence of matter. Matter is the boundary, beyond which the mind cannot pass. Matter furnishes the background for the illumination of the mind, but is not consumed in this illumination. Mind is a product of matter, but matter is more than a product of mind, being perceived also through the five senses and thus brought to our notice. We call real, objective products, or "things themselves" only such products as are revealed to us simultaneously by the senses and the mind.

Reason is a real thing only in so far as it is perceived by the senses. The perceptible actions of reason are revealed in the brain of man as well as in the world outside of it. For are not the effects tangible by which reason transforms nature and life? We see the successes of science with our eyes and grasp them with our hands. It is true that science or reason cannot produce such material effects out of themselves. The world of sense perceptions, the objects outside of the human brain, must be given. But what thing is there that has any effects "in itself?" In order that light may shine, that the sun may warm, and revolve in its course, there must be space and other things which may be lighted and warmed and passed. In order that my table may have color, there must be light and eyes. And everything else which my table is besides, it can be only in contact with other things. Its being is just as manifold as those various contacts or relations. In short, the world consists only in its interrelations. Any thing that is torn out of its relations with the world ceases to exist. A thing is anything "in itself" only because it is something for other things, by acting or appearing in connection with something else.

If we wish to regard the world in the light of the "thing itself," we shall easily see that the world "itself" and the world as it appears, the world of phenomena, differ only in the same way in which the whole differs from its component parts. The world "itself" is nothing else but the sum total of its phenomena. The same holds good of that part of the world phenomena which we call reason, spirit, faculty of thought. Although we distinguish between the faculty of thought and its phenomena or manifestations, yet the faculty of thought "itself," or "pure" reason, exists in reality only in the sum total of its manifestations. Seeing is the physical existence of the faculty of sight. We possess the whole only by means of its parts, and we can possess reason, like all other things, only by the help of its effects, by its various thoughts. But we repeat that reason does not precede thought in the order of time. On the contrary thoughts generated by perceptible objects serve as a basis for the development of the concept of the faculty of thought. Just as the understanding of the world movements has taught us that the sun is not revolving around the earth, so the understanding of the thought process tells us that it is not the faculty of thought which creates thought, but vice versa, that the concept of this faculty is created out of a series of concrete thoughts. Hence the faculty of thought practically exists only as the sum total of our thoughts, just as the faculty of sight exists only through the sum of the things that we see.

These thoughts, this practical reason, serve as the material out of which our brain manufactures the concept of "pure" reason. Reason is necessarily impure in practice, which means that it must connect itself with some object. Pure reason, or abstract reason without any special content, cannot be anything else but the general characteristic of all concrete reasoning processes. We possess this general nature of reason in two ways: In an impure state, that is as practical and concrete phenomenon, consisting of the sum of our real perceptions, and in a pure state, that is theoretically or abstractly, in the concept. The phenomenon of reason is distinguished from reason "itself" just as the real animals are distinguished from the concept of the animal.

Every actual reasoning process is based on some real object which has many qualities like all things in nature. The faculty of thought extracts from this many-sided object those properties which are general or common with it. A mouse and an elephant, as the objects of our reasoning activity, lose their differences in the general animal concept. Such a concept combines many things under one uniform point of view, it develops one general idea out of many concrete things. Since understanding is the general or common quality of all reasoning processes, it follows that reason in general, or the general nature of the reasoning process, consists in abstracting the general ideal character from any concrete thing perceptible by the help of the senses.

Reason being unable to exist without some objects outside of itself, it is understood that we can perceive "pure" reason, or reason "itself," only by its practical manifestations. We cannot find reason without objects outside of it with which it comes in contact and produces thought, any more than we can find any eyes without light. And the manifestations of reason are as varied as the objects which supply its material. It is plain, then, that reason has no separate existence "in itself," but that on the contrary the concept of reason is formed out of the material supplied by the senses.

Mental processes appear only in connection with perceptible phenomena. These processes are themselves phenomena of sense perception which, in connection with a brain process, produce the concept of the faculty of thought "itself." If we analyze this concept, we find that "pure" reason consists in the activity of producing general ideas out of concrete materials, which include so-called immaterial thoughts. In other words, reason may be characterized as an activity which seeks for unity in every multiplicity and equalizes all contrasts whether it deals with the many different sides and parts of one or of more objects. All these different statements describe the same thing in different words, so that the reader may not cling to the empty word, but grasp the living concept, the manifold object, in its general nature.

Reason, we said, exists in a "pure" state as the development of the general out of the special, of the abstract out of concrete sense perceptions. This is the whole content of pure reason, of scientific understanding, of consciousness. And by the terms "pure" and "whole" we simply indicate that we mean the general content of the various thought processes, the general form of reason. Apart from this general abstract form, reason, like all other things, has also its concrete, special, sense form which we perceive directly through our experience. Hence our entire process of consciousness consists in the experience of the senses, that is in the physical process, and its understanding. Understanding is the general reflection of any object.

Consciousness, as the Latin root of the word indicates, is the knowledge of being in existence. It is a form, or a quality, of existence which differs from other forms of being in that it is aware of its existence. Quality cannot be explained, but must be experienced. We know by experience that consciousness includes along with the knowledge of being in existence the difference and contradiction between subject and object, thinking and being, between form and content, between phenomenon and essential thing, between attribute and substance, between the general and the concrete. This innate contradiction explains the various terms applied to consciousness, such as the organ of abstraction, the faculty of generalization or unification, or in contradistinction thereto the faculty of differentiation. For consciousness generalizes differences and differentiates generalities. Contradiction is innate in consciousness, and its nature is so contradictory that it is at the same time a differentiating, a generalizing, and an understanding nature. Consciousness generalizes contradiction. It recognizes that all nature, all being, lives in contradictions, that everything is what it is only in cooperation with its opposite. Just as visible things are not visible without the faculty of sight, and vice versa the faculty of sight cannot see anything but what is visible, so contradiction must be recognized as something general which pervades all thought and being. The science of understanding, by generalizing contradiction, solves all concrete contradictions.

III
The Nature of Things

In so far as the faculty of understanding is a physical object, the knowledge of its nature is a matter of physical science. But in so far as we understand all things by the help of this faculty, the science of understanding becomes metaphysics. Inasmuch as the scientific analysis of reason reverses the current conception of its nature, this specific understanding necessarily reverses our entire world philosophy. With the understanding of the nature of reason, we arrive at the long sought understanding of the "nature of things."

We wish to know, understand, conceive, recognize all things in their very nature, not in their outward appearance. Science seeks to understand the nature of things, or their true essence, by means of their manifestations. Every thing has its own special nature, and this nature is not seen, or felt, or heard, but solely perceived by the faculty of thought. This faculty explores the nature of all things just as the eye explores all that is visible in things. Just as the nature of sight is understood by the theory of vision, so the nature of things in general is understood by the theory of understanding.

It is true that it sounds contradictory to say that the nature of a thing does not appear to the eye, but to the faculty of thought, and at the same time to imply that the opposite of appearance, nature, should appear. But we here refer to the nature of a thing as a phenomenon in the same way in which we referred to the mind as a perception of the senses, and we shall demonstrate further on that every being is a phenomenon, and every phenomenon is more or less of an essential thing.

We have seen that the faculty of thought requires for its vital activity an object, or raw material. The effect of reasoning is seen in science, no matter whether we understand the term science in its narrow classical sense or in its broadest meaning of any kind of knowledge. The phenomena of sense perception constitute the general abject or material of science. Sense perceptions arise from infinite circulation of matter. The universe and all things in it consist of transformations of matter which take place simultaneously and consecutively in space and time. The universe is in every place and at any time itself, new, and present for the first time. It arises and passes away, passes and arises under our very hands. Nothing remains the same, only the infinite change is constant, and even the change varies. Every particle of time and space brings new changes. It is true that the materialist believes in the permanency, eternity, indestructibility of matter. He teaches us that not the smallest particle of matter has ever been lost in the world, that matter simply changes its forms eternally, but that its nature lasts indestructibly through all eternity. And yet, in spite of all distinctions between matter itself and its perishable form, the materialist is on the other hand more inclined than any one else to dwell on the identity of matter and its forms. Inasmuch as the materialist speaks ironically of formless matter and matterless forms, in the same breath with perishable forms of imperishable matter, it is plain that materialism is not informed any more than idealism as to the relation of content to form, of a phenomenon to the essential nature of its subject. Where do we find such eternal, imperishable, formless matter? In the world of sense perceptions we never meet anything but forms of perishable matter. It is true that there is matter everywhere, wherever anything passes away, something new instantly arises. But nowhere has any homogeneous, unchangeable matter enduring without any form, ever been discovered. Even a chemically indivisible element is only a relative unit in its actual existence, and in extension of time as well as in extension through space it varies simultaneously and consecutively as much as any organic individual which also changes only its concrete forms, but remains the same in its general nature from beginning to end. My body changes continually its fleshy tissue, bones, and every other particle belonging to it, and yet it always remains the same. What constitutes, then, this body which is distinguished from its transient form? It is the sum total, in a generalized way, of all its varied concrete forms. Eternal and imperishable matter exists in reality only as the sum total of its perishable forms. The statement that matter is imperishable cannot mean anything but that there will always and everywhere be matter. It is just as true to say that matter is imperishable and merely changes its forms, as it is to say that matter exists only in its changing forms, that it is matter which changes and that only the change is eternal. The terms "changeable matter" and "material change" are after all only different expressions for the same thing.

In the practical world of sense perceptions, there is nothing permanent, nothing homogeneous, nothing beyond nature, nothing like a "thing itself." Everything is changing, passing, phantomlike, so to say. One phantom is chased by another. "Nevertheless," says Kant, "things are also something in themselves, for otherwise we should have the absurd contradiction that there could be phenomena without things that produce them." But no! A phenomena is no more and no less different from the thing which produces it than the the stretch of a twenty-mile road is different from the road itself. Or we may distinguish between a knife and its blade and handle, but we know that that there would be no knife if there were no blade and no handle. The essential nature of the universe is change. Phenomena appear, that is all.

The contradiction between the "thing itself;" or its essence, and its outward appearance is fully solved by a complete critique of reason which arrives at the understanding that the human faculty of thought may generalize any number of varied sense perceptions under one uniform point of view, by singling out the general and equivalent forms and thus regarding everything it may meet as a concrete part of one and the same whole.

In other words, the relative and transient forms perceived by our senses serve as raw material for our brain activity, which abstracts the general likeness out of the concrete forms and systematizes or classifies them for our consciousness. The infinite variety of sense perceptions passes in review before our subjective mind, and it constructs out of the multiplicity the unity, out of the parts the whole, out of the phenomena the essential nature, out of the perishable the imperishable, out of the attributes the subject. The essence, the nature of things, the "thing itself" is an ideal, a spiritual conception. Consciousness knows how to make sums out of different units. It can take any number of units for its' sums. The entire multiplicity of the universe is theoretically conceived as one unit. On the other hand, every abstract sum consists in reality of an infinite number of sense perceptions. Where do we find any indivisible unit outside of our abstract conceptions? Two halves, four fourths, eight eighths, or an infinite number of separate parts form the raw material out of which the mind fashions the mathematical unit. This book, its leaves, its letters, or their parts, are they units? Where do I begin, where do I stop? In the same way, I may call a library with many volumes, a house, a farm, and finally the whole universe, a unit. Is not everything a part, is not every part a thing? Is the color of a leaf less of a thing than that leaf itself? Perhaps some would call the color simply an attribute and the leaf its substance, because there might be a leaf without color, but no color without a leaf. But as surely as we exhaust a heap of sand by scattering it, just as surely do we remove all the substance of a leaf when we take away its attributes one after the other. Color is only the sum of reactions of leaf, light, and eye, and so is all the rest of the matter of a leaf an aggregate of interactions. In the same way in which our reason deprives a leaf of its color attributes and sets it apart as a "thing itself," may we continue to deprive that leaf of all its other attributes, and in so doing we finally take away everything that makes the leaf. Color is in its nature no less a substance than the leaf itself, and the leaf is no less an attribute than its color. As the color is an attribute of a leaf, so a leaf is an attribute of a tree, a tree an attribute of the earth, the earth an attribute of the universe. The universe is the substance, substance in general, and all other substances are but its attributes. And this world-substance reveals the fact that the nature of things, the "thing itself" as distinguished from its manifestations, is only a concept of the mind.

In its universal search from the attribute to the substance, from the relative to the absolute, from the appearance of things to the true things, the mind finally arrives at the understanding that the substance is nothing but a sum of attributes collected by brain activity, and that the mind itself, or reason, is a substantial being which creates abstract mental units out of a multitude of sense perceptions and conceives of the universe as an absolute whole, as an independent "thing itself," by adding all its transient manifestations. In turning away full of dissatisfaction from attributes, searching restlessly after the substance, throwing aside phenomena, and forever groping for truth, for the nature of things, for the "thing itself," and in finally realizing that this substantial truth is merely the sum of all so-called untruths, the totality of all phenomena, the mind proves itself to be the creator of the abstract concept of substance. But it did not create this concept out of nothing. On the contrary, it generated the concept of a world substance out of attributes, it derived truth out of manifestations of things.

The idealist conception that there is an abstract nature behind phenomena which materialises itself in them, is refuted by the understanding that this hidden nature does not dwell in the world outside of the human mind, but in the brain of man. But since the brain differentiates between phenomena and their nature, between the concrete and the general, only by means of sense perception, it cannot be denied that the distinction between phenomena and their nature is well founded; only the essential nature of things is not found back of phenomena, but by means of phenomena. This nature is materially existent and our faculty of thought is a real and natural one.

It is true of spiritual things as well as of physical ones, in fact it is true of all things, metaphysically speaking, that they are what they are, not "in themselves," not in their abstract nature, but in contact with other things, in reality. In this sense one might say that things are not what they seem, but manifest themselves because they are existent, and they manifest themselves in as many different ways as there are other things with which they enter into relations of time and space. But the statement that things are not what they seem requires, in order to be rightly understood, the modification that whatever manifests itself, exists in nature, and its existence is limited by its manifestations. "We cannot perceive heat itself," says a book on physics written by Professor Koppe, "we merely conclude from its manifestations that it is present in nature." Thus reasons a naturalist who seeks to understand a thing by practical and diligent study of its manifestations, but who seeks refuge in the speculative belief in a hidden "thing itself" whenever a lack of understanding of the fundamentals of logic embarrasses him. We, on the contrary, conclude that there is no such thing as "heat itself," since it cannot be found, in nature, and we conceive of heat as effects of matter which the human brain translated into the conception of "heat itself." Because science was, perhaps, as yet unable to analyse this conception, the professor says we cannot perceive the natural object which gives rise to this conception. "Heat itself" is simply composed of the sum total of its manifold effects, and there is nothing else to it. The faculty of thought generalizes this variety of effects under the concept of heat in general. The analysis of this conception, the discovery of the general character of the various manifestations of heat, is the function of inductive science. But the conception of heat separated from its effects is a speculative idea, similar to Lichtenberg's knife without handle and blade.

The faculty of thought in touch with sense perceptions produces the nature of things. But it produces them no more independently of things outside than do the eye, the ears or any other sense of man. It is not the "things themselves" which we see or feel, but their effects on our eyes, hands, etc. The faculty of reason to generalize different perceptions of the eye permits us to distinguish between concrete sights and sight in general. The faculty of thought conceives of any concrete sight as an object of sight in general. It furthermore distinguishes between subjective and objective sight perceptions, the latter being sights which are visible not alone to the individual eye, but to eyesight in general. Even the visions of a spiritualist, or such subjective impressions as forked lightning, circles of fire, caused by excited blood of closed eyes, serve as objects for the critical consciousness. A glittering object revealed by bright sunlight miles away is no more and no less tangible in substance, no more and no less true, than any optical illusion. A man whose ear is tingling hears something, though it is not the tinkling of bells. Every sense perception is an object, and every object is a sense perception. The object of any subjective mind is a passing manifestation, and every objective perception is but a perishable subject. The object of observation may exist in a more tangible, less approachable, more stable, or more general form, but it is not a "thing itself," It may be perceived not alone by my eyes, but also by those of others, not by the eyes, but also by the feeling, the hearing, the taste, etc. And it may be noticed not alone by men, but also by other objects. But nevertheless it appears only as a manifestation, it is different in different places, it is not today what it is tomorrow. Every existence is relative, in touch with other things, and entering into different relations of time and space with them.

Every sense perception is an actual and natural object. Truth exists in the form of natural phenomena, and whatever is, is true. Substance and attribute are only terms for certain relations. They are not contradictions, and, as a matter of fact, all contradictions disappear before our faculty of generalization and differentiation. For this faculty reconciles all contradictions by finding a general quality in all differences, Existence, or universal truth, is the general object, the raw material, of the faculty of thought. This material is of the utmost variety and supplied by the senses. The senses reveal to us the substance of the universe in the forms of concrete qualities, in other words, the nature of perceptible matter is revealed to the faculty of thought through a variety of concrete forms. It is not perceived as a general essence, but only through interdependent phenomena. Out of the interdependence of the sense perceptions with our faculty of thought there arise quantities, general concepts, things, true perceptions, or understood truths.

Essence and truth are two terms for the same thing. Truth, or the essence and nature of things, is a theoretical concept. As we have seen, we receive impressions of things in two ways, viz., a sense impression and a mental impression, the one practical, the other theoretical. Practice furnishes us with the sense impression, theory with the mental nature of things.

Practice is the premise of theory, sense perception the premise of the nature which is also called the truth. The same truth manifests itself in practice either simultaneously or consecutively in the same place or in different places. It exists theoretically as a homogeneous conception.

Practice, phenomena, sense perceptions, are absolute qualities, that is to say they have no quantitative limitation, they are not restricted by time or space. They are absolute and infinite qualities. The qualities of a thing are as infinite as its parts. On the other hand, the work of the faculty of thought, of theory, creates at will an infinite number of quantities and it conceives every quality of sense perceptions in the form of quantities, as the essential nature of things, as truths. Every conception has a quality of same sense perception for its object. Every object can be conceived by the faculty of thought only as a quantitative unit, as true nature, as truth.

The faculty of thought produces in contact with sense perceptions that which manifests itself as true nature, as a general truth. A primitive concept accomplishes this at first only instinctively, while a scientific concept is a conscious and voluntary repetition of this primitive act. Scientific understanding wanting to know an object, such as for instance heat, is not hunting after the phenomena themselves. It does not aim to see or hear how heat melts iron or wax, how it benefits in one case or injures in another, how it makes eggs solid or ice liquid, nor does it concern itself with the difference between the heat of an animal, of the sun, or of a stove. All these things are from the point of view of the faculty of understanding, only effects, phenomena, qualities. It desires to get at the essence, the true nature of things, it strives to find a general law, a concise scientific extract, of things seen, heard, and felt. The abstract nature of things cannot be a tangible object. It is a concept of theory, of science, of the faculty of thought. The understanding of heat consists in singling out that which is common to all phenomena of heat, which is essential or true for all heat.

Practically, the nature of heat consists of the sum total of all its manifestations, theoretically in its concept, scientifically in the analysis of this concept. To analyze the concept of heat means to ascertain that which is common to all manifestations of heat.

The general nature of the thing is its true nature, the general quality its true quality. We define rain more truly as being wet than as being fertilizing, because it gives moisture wherever it falls, while it fertilizes only under certain circumstances and in certain places. My true friend is one who is constant and loyal to me all my life under all circumstances. Of course, we must not believe in any absolute and unconditional friendship any more than in any absolute and eternal truth. Perfectly true, perfectly universal, is only the general existence, the universe, the absolute quantity. But the real world is absolutely relative, absolutely perishable, an infinity of manifestations, an infinity of qualities. All truths are simply parts of this world, partial truths. Semblance and truth flow dialectically into one another like hard and soft, good and bad, right and wrong, but at the same time they remain different. Even though I know that there is no rain which is "fertile in itself," and no friend who is true in an absolute sense, I may nevertheless refer to a certain rain as fertile in relation to certain crops, and I may distinguish between my more or less true friends.

The universe is the truth. The universe is that which is universal, that is, things which exist and are perceived. The general mark of truth is existence, because universal existence is truth. Now, existence is not a general abstraction, but a reality in the concrete form of sense perceptions. The world of sense perceptions has its true and perceptible existence in the passing and manifold manifestations of nature and life. Therefore all manifestations are recognized as relative truths, all truths as concrete and temporal manifestations. The manifestation of practice is considered as a truth in theory, and vice versa, the truth of theory is manifested in practice. Opposites are mutually relative. Truth and error differ only comparatively, in volume of degree, like being and seeming, life and death, light and dark, like all other opposites in the world. It is a matter of course that all things of this world are worldly, consequently are of the same matter, the same nature, the same family, the same quality. In other words, every volume of perceptible manifestation forms in contact with the human faculty of thought, a being, a truth, a general thing. For our consciousness, every particle of dust as well as every dust cloud, or any other mass of material manifestations, is on the one hand an abstract "thing in itself," and on the other a passing phenomenon of the absolute object, the universe. Inside of this universe the various manifestations are systematized or generalized at will and on purpose by means of our mind. The chemical element is as much a many-sided system as the organic cell or the whole vegetable kingdom. The smallest and the largest being is divided into individuals, species, families, classes, etc. This systematization, this generalization, this generation of beings is continued in an ascending scale up to the infinity of the universe, and in the descending scale down to the infinity of the parts. In the eyes of the faculty of thought all qualities become abstract things, all things relative qualities.

Every thing, every sense perception, no matter how subjective or short-lived it may be, is true, is a certain part of truth. In other words, the truth exists, not only in the general existence, but every concrete existence has also its own distinct generality or truth.

Every object, whether it be a mere passing idea, or a volatile scent, or some tangible matter, constitutes a sum of manifold phenomena. The faculty of thought turns various quantities into one, discerns the equality in different things, seeks the unity in the multiplicity. Mind and matter have at least actual existence in common. Organic nature agrees with inorganic nature in being material. It is true that there are wide divergences between man, monkey, elephant, and plants attached to the soil, but even greater differences are reconciled under the term "organism," However much a stone may differ from a human heart, thinking reason will discover innumerable similarities in them. They at least agree in being matter, they are both visible, tangible, and may be weighed, etc. Their differences are as manifold as their likenesses. Solomon truly says that there is nothing new under the sun, and Schiller also says truly that the world grows old and again grows young. What abstract thing, being, existence, generality is there that is not manifold in its sense manifestations, and individually different from all other things? There are no two drops of water alike. I am now in many respects different from what I was an hour ago, and the likeness between my brother and myself is only relatively greater than the likeness between a watch and an oyster. In short, the faculty of thought is a faculty of absolute generalization, it classes all things without exception under one head, it comprises and understands everything uniformly, while sense perceptions show absolutely everything in a different, new and individual light. If we apply this metaphysics* to our study, the faculty of thought, we see that its functions, like all other things, are material manifestations, which are all equally true. All manifestations of the mind, all ideas, opinions, errors, partake of a certain truth, all of them have a kernel of truth. Just as inevitably as a painter derives all forms of his creation from perceptible objects around him, so are all ideas, images of true things, theories of true objects. So far as perceptions are perceptions, it is a matter of course that all perceptions perceive something. So far as knowledge is knowledge, it requires no explanation that all knowledge knows something. This follows from the rule of identity, according to which a equals a, or from the rule of contradiction, according to which 100 is not 1,000.

All perceptions are thoughts. One might claim, on the other hand, that all thoughts are not perceptions. One might define "perceiving" as a special kind of thought, as real objective thought in distinction from supposing, believing, or imagining. But it cannot be denied that all thoughts have a common nature, in spite of their many differences. Thought is treated in the court of the faculty of thought like all other things, it is made uniform. No matter how different the thoughts I had yesterday may be from those I have to-day, no matter how much the thoughts of different human beings may vary at different times, no matter how clearly we may distinguish between such thoughts as those expressed by the terms idea, conception, judgment, conclusion, impression, etc., they each and all possess the same common and universal nature, because all of them are manifestations of mind.

It follows, then, that the difference between true and erroneous thoughts, between understanding and misunderstanding, like all other differences, is only relative. A thought "in itself" is neither false nor true, it is either of these only in relation to some other object. Thoughts, conceptions, theories, natures, truths, all have this in common that they belong to some object, we have seen that any object is a part of the multiplicity of sense perceptions in the world outside of our brains. After as much of the universal being as constitutes the object which is to be understood has been defined by some customary term of language, truth is to be found in the discovery of the general nature of this perceptible part of being.

The perceptible parts of being which constitute the things of this world have not only a semblance and manifestation, but also a true nature which is given by means of their manifestation. The nature of things is as infinite in number as the world of sense perceptions is infinitely divisible in space and time. Every part of any phenomenon has its own nature, every special phenomenon has its general truth. A phenomenon is perceived in touch with the senses, while the true or essential nature of things is perceived in contact with our faculty of thought. In this way we find ourselves face to face with the necessity of speaking here, where the nature of things is up for discussion, simultaneously of the faculty of thought, and on the other hand of dealing with the nature of things when the faculty of thought is our main subject.

We said at the outset: The criterion of truth includes the criterion of reason. Truth, like reason, consists in developing a general concept, or an abstract theory, from a given sum of sense perceptions. Therefore it is not abstract truth which is the criterion of true understanding, but we rather refer to that understanding as being true which produces the truth, or the general hall-mark of any concrete object. Truth must be objective, that is to say it must be the truth about some concrete object. Perceptions cannot be true to themselves, they are true only in relation to some definite object, and to some outside facts. The work of understanding consists in the abstraction of the general hall-mark from concrete objects. The concrete is the measure of the general, the standard of truth. Whatever is, is true, no matter how much or how little true it may be. Once we have found existence, its general nature follows as truth itself. The difference between that which is more or less general, between being and seeming, between truth and error, is limited to definite conditions, for it presupposes the relation to some special object. Whether a perception is true or false will, therefore, depend not so much on perception as on the scope of the question which perception tries to solve of its own accord or which it is called upon to solve by external circumstances. A perfect understanding is possible only within definite limits. A perfect truth is one which is always aware of its imperfection. For instance, it is perfectly true that all bodies have weight only because the concept of "body" has previously been limited to things which have weight. After reason has assigned the conception of "body in general" to things of various weights, it is no longer a matter for surprise to find that bodies must inevitably have weight. Once it is assumed that the term "bird" was abstracted exclusively from flying animals, we may be sure that all birds fly, whether they are in heaven, on earth, or in any other place. And to explain this we do not require the belief in *a priori* conceptions which are supposed to differ from empirical conceptions by their strict necessity and generality. Truths are valid only under certain conditions, and under certain conditions errors may be true. It is a true perception that the sun is shining, provided we understand that the sky is not covered by clouds. And it is no less true that a straight stick becomes crooked in flowing water, provided we understand that this truth is an optical one.

Truth is that which is common or general to our reasoning faculty within a given circle of sense perceptions. To call within a definite circle of sense perceptions that which is exceptional or special the ride or the general, is error.

Error, the opposite of truth, arises when the faculty of thought, or consciousness, inadvertently or shortsightedly and without previous experience concedes to certain phenomena a more general scope than is supported by the senses, for instance when it hastily attributes to what is in fact only an optical existence, a supposed plastic existence also.

The judgment of error is a prejudice. Truth and error, understanding and misunderstanding, knowing and not knowing, have their common habitation in the faculty of thought which is the organ of science. Thought at large is the general expression of experienced facts perceived by the senses, and it includes errors as well. Error is distinguished from truth in that the former assigns to any definite fact of which it is a manifestation, a wider and more general existence than is supported by sense perceptions and experience. Unwarranted assumption is the nature of error. A glass bead does not become a counterfeit, until it pretends to be a genuine pearl.

Schleiden says of the eye: "When the excited blood expands the veins and presses on the nerves, we feel it in the fingers as pain, we see it in the eyes as forked lightning. And thus we obtain the irrefutable proof that our conceptions are free creations of the mind, that we do not perceive the external world as it really is, but that its reflex actions on us simply give rise to a peculiar brain activity, on our part. The products of this activity are frequently connected with certain processes of the external world, but frequently they are not. We close our eyes and we see a circle of light, but there is in reality no shining body: It is easy to see that this may be a great and dangerous source of errors of all kinds. From the teasing forms of a misty moonlight night to the threatening and insanity-producing visions of the believer in ghosts we meet a series of illusions which are not derived from any direct processes of external nature, but belong to the field of the free activity of the mind which is subject to error. It requires great judgment and wide education, before the mind learns to break away from all its own errors and to control them. Reading in general seems so easy, and yet it is a difficult art. It is only by degrees that the mind learns to understand which of the messages of the nerves may be trusted and used as a basis for conceptions. The light, if we consider it entirely by itself, is not clear, not yellow, nor blue nor red. The light is a movement of a very fine and everywhere diffused substance, the ether."

The beautiful world of light and splendor, of color and form, is supposed not to be a perception of something which really is. "Through the thick covering of the grape arbor, a ray of sunlight undulates into the cooling shadows. You think you see the ray of light itself, but what you really see is nothing but a flock of dust particles." The truth about light and color is said to be that they are "waves rushing through ether in restless succession at the rate of 100,000 miles per second." This true physical nature of light and color is supposed to be so illusive, that "it required the sharp intellects of the greatest thinkers to reveal to us this true nature of light. We find that every one of our senses is susceptible only to definite external influences, and that the stimulation of different senses produces different conceptions in our mind. Thus the sense organs are the mediators between the external soulless world (undulations of the ether), which is revealed to us by science, and the beautiful world of sense perceptions in which we find ourselves with our minds."

Schleiden thus gives an illustration of the fact that there is still a great deal of embarrassment, even in our times, when the understanding of these two worlds is under discussion, that there is still much helpless groping to explain the connection between the world of thought, of knowledge or science, which is in this case represented by undulations of the ether, and between the world of our five senses, represented by the bright and colored lights of the eyes or of reality. At the same time this illustration shows how queer the traditional survivals of speculative philosophy sound in the mouth of a modern scientist. The confused condition of this mode of thought is seen in the distinction between "an external sense-perceived world of science and another one, in which we find ourselves with our minds." The distinction between the senses and the mind, between theory and practice, between the special and the general, between truth and error, has been noticed by such thinkers, but they have no solution for it. They know there is something missing, but they do not know where to look for it, and therefore they are confused.

The great scientific achievement of the XIXth century consists in the victory over speculation, over knowledge without sense perception, in the delivery of the senses from the thralldom of such knowledge, and in the foundation of empirical investigation. To acknowledge the theoretical value of this achievement means to come to an understanding about the source of error. Contrary to a philosophy that tries to discover truth with the mind, and error with the senses, we seek for truth with the senses and regard the mind as the source of errors. The belief in certain messages of the nerves which are alone worthy of confidence and which can be understood only by degrees without any specific mark of distinction, is a superstition. Let us have confidence in all testimonials of the senses. There is nothing false to be separated from the genuine. The supernatural mind idea is the only deceiver whenever it undertakes to disregard the sense perceptions, and, instead of being the interpreter of the senses, tries to enlarge their statements and repeat what has not been dictated. The eye, in seeing forked lightning or radiant circles when the blood is excited or a pressure exerted on it, perceives no more errors than it does in perceiving any other manifestation of the external world. It is our faculty of thought which makes a mistake, by regarding without further inquiry such subjective events as objective bodies. One who sees ghosts does not commit any mistake, until he claims that his personal apparition is a general phenomenon, until he prematurely takes something for an experience which he has not experienced. Error is an offense against the law of truth which prescribes to our consciousness that it must remember the limits within which a perception is true, or general. Error makes out of something special a generality, out of a predicate a subject, and takes the part for the whole. Error makes *a priori* conclusions, while truth, its opposite, arrives at understanding by *a posteriori* reasoning.

A priori and *a posteriori* understanding are related in the same way as philosophy and natural science, taking the latter in the widest meaning of the term, that of science in general. The contrast between believing and knowing is duplicated in that between philosophy and natural science. Speculative philosophy, like religion, lives on faith. The modern world has transformed faith into science. The reactionists in politics who demand that science retrace its steps desire its return to faith. The content of faith is acquired without exertion. Faith makes *a priori* perceptions, while science arrives at its knowledge by hard *a posteriori* study. To give up faith means to give up taking things easy. And to confine science to *a posteriori* knowledge means to decorate it with the characteristic mark of modern times, work.

It is not a result of scientific study, but merely a freak of philosophy on the part of Schleiden to deny the reality and truth of light phenomena, to call them fantasmagoria created by the free play of the mind. His superstitious belief in philosophical speculation misleads him into abandoning the scientific method of induction and speaking of "waves rushing through ether in restless succession at the rate of 160,000 miles per hour" as being the real and true nature of light and color, in contradistinction to the color phenomena of light. The perversion of this mode of procedure becomes evident by his referring to the material world of the eyes as a "creation of the mind" and to the undulations of the ether, revealed by the "sharp intellect of the greatest thinkers as physical nature."

The truth of science maintains the same relation to the sense perception that the general does to the special, waves of light, the so-called truth of light and color, represent the "true" nature of light only in so far as they represent what is common to all light phenomena, whether they are white, yellow, blue, or any other color. The world of the mind, or of science finds its raw material, its premise, its proof, its beginning, and its boundary in sense perception.

When we have learned that the nature, or the truth, of things is not back of their phenomena, but can be perceived only by the help of phenomena, and that it does not exist "in itself," but only in connection with the faculty of understanding, that the nature is separated from the phenomena only by thought; and when we see on the other hand, that the faculty of understanding does not derive conceptions out of itself, but only out of their relations with some phenomenon; then this discussion of the "nature of things" is an evidence that the nature of the faculty of thought is a conception which we have obtained from its sense manifestations. To understand that the faculty of thought, although universal in the choice of its objects, is nevertheless limited in that it requires some object; to recognize that the true thought process, that is to say the thought with a scientific result, differs from unscientific thinking by consciously attaching itself to some external object; to realize that truth, or universality, is not perceived "in itself," but can be perceived only by means of some given object; this frequently varied statement reveals the nature of the faculty of thought. This statement re-appears at the end of every chapter, because all special truths, all special chapters, serve only to demonstrate the general chapter of universal truth.

IV

The Practice of Reason in Physical Science

Although we know that reason is attached to perceptible matter, to physical objects, so that science can never be anything else but the science of the physical, still we may, according to the prevailing ideas and usage of language, separate physics from logic and ethics, and thus distinguish them as different forms of science. The problem is then to demonstrate that in physics as well as in logic, as also in ethics, the general or intellectual perceptions can be practically obtained only on the basis of concrete perceptible facts.

This practice of reason, to generate thought from matter, to arrive at understanding by sense perceptions, to produce the general out of the concrete, has been universally accepted in physical investigation, but only in practice. The inductive method is employed, and one is aware of this fact, but it is not understood that the nature of inductive science is the nature of science in general, of reason. The process of thought is misunderstood.

Physical science lacks the theory of understanding and for this reason often falls out of its practical step. The faculty of thought is still an unknown, mysterious, mystical being for natural science. Either it confounds the function with the organ, the mind with the brain, as do the materialists, or it thinks with the idealists that the faculty of thought is an imperceptible object outside of its field. We see modern investigators marching toward their goal with firm and uniform steps, so far as physical matters are concerned. But they aimlessly grope around in the abstract relations of these things. The inductive method has been practically adopted by natural science and its successes have secured a great reputation for it. On the other hand, the speculative method has become discredited by its failures. There is, however, no conscious understanding of these various methods of thought. We see the men of physical research, when they are outside of their special field, offer lawyer-like speculations in lieu of scientific facts. While they arrive at the special troths of their chosen fields by sense perceptions, they still pretend to derive speculative truths out of the depths of their own minds.

Listen to the following statements of Alexander von Humboldt, which he makes in the initial argument of his "Cosmos" in regard to speculation: "The most important result of physical research by sense perception is this: that it finds the element of unity in a multitude of forms; that it grasps all the individual manifestations offered by the discoveries of recent times, carefully scrutinizes and distinguishes them; yet does not succumb under their mass; that it fulfills the sublime mission of the human being, of understanding the nature of things which is hidden under the cover of phenomena. In this way our aim reaches beyond the narrow limits of the senses, and we may succeed in grasping the nature by controlling the raw material of empirical observation through ideas. In my observations of the scientific treatment of general cosmic phenomena, I am not deriving unity out of a few fundamental principles found by speculative reason. My work is the expression of a thoughtful observation of empirical phenomena seen as one and the same nature . . . I am not going to venture into a field which is foreign to me. What I call physical cosmology does not, therefore, aspire to the rank of a rational science of nature. True to the character of my former occupation and writings, which were devoted to experiments, measurements, and investigations of facts, I confine myself in this work to empirical observations. It is the only ground on which I can move with a measure of security." In the same breath Humboldt says that "without the earnest desire for the knowledge of concrete facts any great and universal world philosophy would be merely castle in the air" and in another place "that an understanding of the universe by speculative and introspective reason would represent a still more sublime aim" than understanding by empirical thought. And on page 68 of volume I, he says: "I am far from finding fault with endeavors of others the success of which still remains in doubt, when I have had no practical experience with them."

Now natural science shares with Humboldt the consciousness that the practice of reason in physical research consists exclusively in *perceiving the element of unity in a multitude of forms*. But on the other hand, though it does not always admit its belief in speculative introspection as frankly as Humboldt does, it nevertheless proves that it does not fully understand the practice of science and that it believes; in a metaphysical as well as a physical science by using the speculative method in the treatment of so-called philosophical topics, in which the element of unity is supposed to be discovered by introspective reason instead of an analysis of multiform sense perceptions, and it demonstrates its lack of unity by being unaware of the unscientific character of disagreements, by believing in a metaphysical science outside of the physical domain.

The relations between phenomenon and its nature, cause and effect, matter and force, substance and spirit, are certainly physical ones. But what is there of unity that science teaches about them? Plainly then, the work of science, like that of the farmer, has so far been done only practically, but not scientifically, not with a predetermination of success. Understanding, that is to say the practice of understanding, is well applied in science, I readily admit. But the instrument of this understanding, the faculty of thought, it misunderstood. We find that natural science, instead of applying this faculty scientifically, simply experiments with it. What is the reason for this? Natural science has neglected the critique of reason, the theory of science, logic Just as the handle and the blade of a knife constitute its general content, so we found that the general content of reason was the universal, the general "itself." We know that it does not produce this content out of itself, but out of given objects, and these objects are the sum of all natural or physical things. The object of reason is, therefore, an infinite, unlimited, absolute quantity. This infinite quantity manifests itself in finite quantities. In the treatment of relatively small quantities of nature the true essence of reason, the true method of understanding, is well recognizes it remains to be demonstrated that the great relation of the world, the treatment of which is still doubtful are likewise intelligible by the same method. Cause and effect, mind and matter, matter and force, are such great world problems, and they are of a physical character. We shall demonstrate that the most general distinction between reason and its object furnishes the key to the solution of the great world problems.

(a) Cause and Effect

"The nature of natural history," says F. W. Bessell, "lies in the fact that it does not consider phenomena as facts in themselves, but looks for their cause The knowledge of nature is thus reduced to the minimum number of facts." But the causes of the phenomena of nature had been investigated even before the age of natural history. The characteristic mark of natural history is not so much that it investigate causes, but that the causes which it investigates have a peculiar nature and a particular quality. Inductive science has materially changed the conception of causes. It has retained the term, but use it in a different sense from that employed by speculation. The naturalist conceives of causes differently within his special field and outside of it; here, outside of his specialty, he frequently indulges in introspective speculation, because he understands science and its cause in a concrete, but not in a general way. The unscientific forces are of a supernatural makeup, they are transcendent spirits, gods, forces, little and big goblins. The original conception of causes is an anthropomorphic one. In a state of inexperience, man measures the objective by a subjective standard, judges the world by himself. Just as he creates things with conscious intent, so he attributes to nature his human manner, imagines the existence of an external and creative cause of the phenomena of sense perception, similar to himself who is the special cause of his own creations. This subjective mood is to blame for the fact that the struggle for objective understanding has so long been in vain. The unscientifically conceived cause is a speculation of the *a priori* kind.

If the term understanding is retained for subjective understanding, then objective science differs from it in that such a science penetrates to the causes of its objects not by faith or introspective speculation, but by experience and induction, not *a priori*, but *a posteriori*. Natural science looks for causes not outside or back of nature's phenomena, but within or by means of them. Modern research seeks no external creator of causes, but rather the immanent system, the method or general mode of the various phenomena as they are given by succession ill time. The unscientifically conceived cause is a "thing in itself," a little god who generates his effects independently and hides behind them. The scientific conception of causes, on the other hand, looks only for the theory of effects, the general element of phenomena. To investigate a cause means then to generalize a variety of phenomena, to arrange the multiplicity of experienced facts under one scientific rule. "The knowledge of nature is thus reduced to the minimum number of facts."

The commonplace and inept knowledge differs from the most exalted, rarest, and newly discovered science in the same way in which a petty and childish superstition differs from the historical superstition of a whole period. For this reason we may well choose our illustrations from our daily circle, instead of looking for them in the so-called higher regions of a remote science. Human common sense had long practiced the investigation of causes by inductive and scientific methods, before science realized that it would have to pursue its higher aims in the same way. Common sense does arrive at the faith in a mysterious cause of speculative reason, just like the naturalist, as soon as it leaves the field of its immediate environment. In order to stand firmly on the ground of real science, every one requires the understanding of the manner in which inductive reason investigates its causes.

To this end let us glance briefly at the outcome of the study of the nature of reason. We know that the faculty of understanding is not a "thing in and by itself," because it becomes real only in contact with some object. But whatever we know of any object, is known not alone through the object, but also through the faculty of reason. Consciousness, like all other being, is relative. Understanding is contact with a variety of objects. To knowledge there is attached distinction, subject and object, variety in unity. Thus things become mutual causes and mutual effects. The entire world of phenomena, of which thought is but a part, a form, is an absolute circle, in which the beginning and end is everywhere and nowhere, in which everything is at the same time essence and semblance, cause and effect, general and concrete. Just as all nature is in the last instance one sole general unity, in view of which all other unities become a multitude, so this same nature, or objectivity, or world of sense perceptions, or whatever else we may call the sum of all phenomena or effects, is the final cause of all things, compared to which all other causes become effects. But we must remember that this cause of all causes is only the sum of all effects, not a transcendental or superior being. Every cause has its effect, every effect causes something.

A cause cannot be physically separated from its effect any more than the visible can be separated from the eye, the taste from the tongue, in brief the general from the concrete. Nevertheless, the faculty of thought may separate the one from the other. We must keep in mind that this separation is a mere formality of thought, although it is a formality which is necessary in order to be reasonable or conscious, in order to act scientifically. The practice or understanding, or scientific practice, derives the concrete from the general, the natural things from nature. But whoever has been behind the scenes, and has looked at the faculty of thought at work, knows that, conversely the general is derived from the concrete, the concept of nature from natural things. The theory of understanding or science teaches us that the antecedent is understood by its consequent, the cause by its effect, while our practical understanding regards the after as a consequence of the before, the effect as a result of the cause. The faculty of understanding, the organ of generalization, regards its opposite, the concrete, as secondary, while the faculty of thought which understands itself regards it as primary. However, the practice of understanding is not to be changed by its theory, nor can it be; the theory intends simply to render the steps of consciousness firm. The scientific farmer differs from the practical farmer, not because he employs theory and method, for both do that, but because he understands the theory, while the practical man theorizes instinctively,

To continue: From a given multitude of facts reason generates truth in general, and out of a succession of forms and transformations it abstracts the true cause. Just as absolute multiplicity is the nature of space, so absolute variability is the nature of time. Every particle of time and space is new, original, and has never been there before. The faculty of thought enables us to find our way through this absolute medley by abstracting general concepts out of the multitude of things in space, and tracing the variations of time to general causes. The entire nature of reason consists in generalizing sense perception in abstracting the common elements out of concrete things. Whoever does not fully understand reason by understanding that it is the organ of generalization forgets that understanding requires an object which must remain something outside of its conception since such object cannot be dissolved by its conception. The being of the reasoning faculty cannot be understood any more than being in general, rather, being is understood when we take it in its generality. Not being itself, but the general element being, is understood by the faculty of thought.

Let us realize, for instance, the process which takes place when reason understands something it did not know before. Think of some peculiar, unexpected and unknown chemical transformation which takes place suddenly and without apparent cause in some mixture. Assume furthermore that the same reaction takes place more frequently after that, until experience demonstrates that this inexplicable change occurs whenever sunlight touches the mixture. This already constitutes a certain understanding of the process. Assume furthermore that subsequent experience teaches us that several other substances have the faculty of producing the same reaction in connection with sunlight. We have then arranged the new reaction in line with a number of phenomena of the same class, that is to say we have enlarged, deepened, completed our understanding of it still more. And if we finally discover that a special part of the sunlight unites with a special element of the mixture and thereby produces this new reaction, we have generalized this experience, or experienced this generalization, in a "pure" state, in other words, the theory of this reaction is complete, reason has solved its problem, and yet it has done nothing more than it did when it classified the animal and vegetable kingdoms in families, genera, species, etc. To find the species, the genus, the sex, etc., of anything means to understand it.

Reason proceeds in the same way when it investigates the causes of certain transformations. Causes are, in the last instance, not noticed and furnished by means of sight, hearing, feeling, not by means of the sense perceptions. They are rather supplied by the faculty of thought. It is true, causes are not the "pure" products of the faculty of thought, but are produced by it in connection with sense perceptions and their material objects. This raw material gives the objective existence to the causes produced by the mind. Just as we demand that a truth should be the truth about some objective phenomenon, so we also demand that a cause should be real, that it should be the cause of some objective effect.

The understanding of any concrete cause is conditioned on the empirical study of its material, while the understanding of any general cause is based on the study of the faculty of reason. In the understanding of concrete causes, the material of study varies, but reason maintains a constant or general attitude. The cause, as a general cause, is a pure conception, and is based on the study of the multiformity of concrete understandings of causes, or on the multiplied study of concrete causes. Hence we are compelled to return to the concrete material of the general concept, to the understanding of concrete causes, if we wish to analyze the concept of a general cause.

When a stone falls into the water and causes ripples on the surface, the stone is no more the cause of the ripples than the liquid condition of the water. If the stone falls on solid substances, it causes no ripples. It is the contact of the falling stone with liquid substances which causes the ripples. The cause is itself an effect, and the effect, the ripples, become cause when they carry a piece of cork ashore. But in either case the cause is based on a mutual effect, on the interaction of the waves with the light condition of the cork.

A stone falling into the water is not a cause "in itself," not a cause in general. We arrive at such cause only, when the faculty of thought uses concrete causes for its raw material and constructs out of then the "pure" concept of the cause in general. A stone falling into the water is only the cause of the subsequent ripples, and it becomes a general cause only through the experience that ripples always follow the falling of a stone into water.

We call cause that which generally precedes a certain manifestation, and effect that which generally follows it, we refer to the stone as the cause of ripples merely, because we know that it always causes them when falling into water. But since ripples sometimes appear without being preceded by the fall of a stone, ripples have another general cause. So far as there is anything general in ripples which precedes them, it is the elasticity of the water itself which is the general cause of ripples. Circular ripples, which are a special form of ripples, are generally preceded by the falling of some body into the water, and this body is then considered as their cause. The cause is always different in proportion and to the extent of the phenomena under consideration.

We cannot ascertain causes by mere introspective reasoning, we cannot derive them out of our head. Matter, materials, sense perceptions are required for this purpose. A definite cause requires a definite material, a definite amount of sense perceptions. In the abstract unity of nature, the variations of matter are represented by the variations of concrete quantities. Every quantity is given in time before and after a certain other quantity, as antecedent and subsequent. The general element of the antecedent is called cause, the general element of the subsequent, effect.

When the wind sways a forest, the yielding character of the forest is as much instrumental in producing this effect as the bending power of the wind. The cause of a thing is its connection with other things. The fact that the same wind leaves rocks and walls standing shows that the cause is not qualitatively different from the effect, but that it is a matter of aggregate effects. If nevertheless science or knowledge determines any special fact to be the cause of any change, that is to say of any succession of phenomena, this cause is no longer regarded as the external creator, but merely as the general mode, the immanent method of succession. A definite cause can be ascertained only when we have under consideration a definite circle, series, or number of changes, the cause of which is to be determined. And within a definite circle of succeeding phenomena, that which generally precedes is their cause.

The wind which sways a forest differs from wind as a general cause only in that the latter has other general effects, inasmuch as it howls in one place, stirs up dust in another, or acts in many different ways. In the special case of the forest, the wind is a cause only in so far as it precedes the swaying of the trees. But in the case of rocks and walls, the solidity precedes the wind and is therefore the general cause of their resistance to the swaying power of the wind. In a still wider circle of hurricane phenomena, a gentle wind may be regarded as a cause of the stability of the objects last mentioned.

The *quantity* or *number* of given objects varies the name of their cause. If a certain company of people return from a walk in a tired condition, this change of condition is just as much due to the physical weakness of the people as to the walk. In other words, a manifestation has in itself no cause which can be separated from it. Everything which was connected with a phenomenon has contributed toward its appearance. In the case of the promenaders, the physical constitution of their bodies has to be considered as well as the physical constitution and length of the road and duration of the walk. If reason is nevertheless called upon to determine the special cause of some concrete change, for instance, of a tired feeling, it is simply a question of determining which one of the various factors has contributed most to that feeling. In this case as well as in all others, the work of reason consists in developing the general from the concrete, that is to say in this case, singling out from a given number of tired sensations that which generally precedes the tired feeling. If most of the promenaders or all of them are found to be tired, the walk will be considered as the cause. But if only a few are tired, the weak constitution of these people will be considered as the general cause of their tired condition.

To use another illustration: If the discharge of a shot frightens some birds, this effect is due to the combined action of the shot and the timidity of the birds. If the majority of the birds fly away, the shot will be considered as the cause. But if the minority fly away, their timidity will be regarded as the cause.

Effects are subsequences. Since all things in nature follow other things and all things have an antecedent and a subsequent, we may call the natural, the real, the sense perceptions absolute effects, having no cause unless we find one with our faculty of thought by systematizing the given material. Causes are mental generalizations of perceptible changes. The supposed relation of cause and effect is a miracle, a creation of something out of nothing. For this reason this relation has been and still is an object of speculative reasoning. The speculative cause creates its effects.

But in reality the effects are the material out of which the brain, or science, forms its causes. The cause concept is a product of reason; not of "pure" reason, but of reason married to the world of sense perceptions.

If Kant maintains that the statement: "Every change has its cause" is an *a priori* truth which we cannot experience because no one can possibly experience all changes, although every one has the irrefutable feeling of the correctness of this statement, we know now that this statement expresses merely the experience that the phenomenon which we call reason recognizes the uniform element in all multiformity. Or in other words, we now know that the development of the general element out of the concrete facts is called reason, thought, or mind. The secure knowledge that every change has its cause is nothing else but the conviction that we are thinking human beings. *Cogito, ergo sum*. I think, therefore I am. We have experienced the nature of our reason instinctively even if we have not analyzed it scientifically. We are as well aware of the faculty of our reason to abstract a cause out of every given change, as we are that every circle is round, that a is equal to a. We know that the general is the product of reason, and reason produces this general thing in contact with every given object. And since all objects before and after a certain other object are temporal changes, it follows that all changes which we as thinking beings experience must have a general antecedent, a cause.

Already the English skeptic Hume felt that true causes are different from assumed causes. According to him the concept of a cause contains nothing but the experience of that which generally precedes a certain phenomenon. Kant rightfully remarks on the other hand that the conception of cause and effect expresses a far more intimate relation than that indicated by a loose and accidental succession, and that the concept of a cause rather comprises that of a certain effect as a necessity and strict general result. Therefore he claimed that there must be something *a priori* in reason which cannot be experienced and which extends beyond experience.

We reply to the materialists who deny all autonomy of the mind and hope to detect causes by experience alone that the general necessity which presupposes the relation of cause and effect represents an impossible experience. And we reply to the idealists: Although reason explores causes which cannot be experienced, this research cannot take place *a priori*, but only *a posteriori*, only on the basis of empirically given effects. It is true that the mind alone discovers the imperceptible and abstract generality, but it does so only within the circle of certain given sense perceptions.

(b) Matter and Mind

The understanding of the general dependence of the faculty of thought on material sense perceptions will restore to objective reality that right which has long been denied to it by ideas and opinions. Nature with its varied concrete phenomena which had been crowded out of human considerations by philosophical and religious imaginings, and which has been scientifically reestablished again on special fields by the development of natural sciences, gains general theoretical recognition by the understanding of the functions of the brain. Hitherto natural science has chosen for its object only special matters, special causes, special forces, but has remained ignorant in general questions of so-called natural philosophy regarding the cause of all things, of matter, of force in general. The actual existence of this ignorance is revealed by that great contradiction between idealism and materialism which pervades all works of science like a red thread.

"May I succeed in this letter in strengthening the conviction that chemistry as an independent science represents one of the most powerful means for the higher cultivation of the mind, that its study is useful not alone for the promotion of the material interests of mankind, but because it permits a deeper penetration of the wonders of creation, with which our existence, our welfare, and our development are intimately connected."

In these words Liebig expresses the prevalent views which have accustomed themselves to look upon material and spiritual differences as absolute opposites. But the untenability of such a distinction is vaguely felt even by the just quoted advocate of this view, who speaks of material interests and of a mental penetration which is the condition for our existence, welfare, and development. But what else does the term material interests mean but the abstract expression of our existence, welfare, and development? Are not these the concrete content of our material interests.

Does he not say explicitly that the penetration of the wonders of creation promotes our material interests? And on the other hand, does not the promotion of our material interests require a penetration on our part of the wonders of creation? In what respect are our material interests different from our mental penetration of things?

The superior, spiritual, ideal, which Liebig in conformity with the views of the world of naturalists opposes to our material interests, is only a special part of those interests. Mental penetration and material interests differ no more than the circle differs from the square. Circles and squares are contrasts, but at the same time they are but different and special classes of form in general.

It has been the custom, especially since the advent of Christian times, to speak contemptuously of material, perceptible, fleshly things which are destroyed by rust and moths. And nowadays people continue on this conservative track, although their antipathy against perceptible reality has long disappeared from their minds and actions. The Christian separation of mind and body has been practically abandoned in the age of natural science. But the theoretical solution of the contradiction, the demonstration that the spiritual is material and the material at the same time spiritual, by which the material interests would be freed from the stigma of inferiority, has not yet been forthcoming.

Modern science is natural science. Science is deemed worthy of its name only in so far as it is natural science. In other words, only that thought is scientific which consciously has real, perceptible, natural things for its object. For this reason representatives and friends of science can not be enemies of nature or of matter. Indeed they are not. But the very existence of science shows that this nature, this world of sense perceptions, this matter or substance, does alone and by itself not satisfy us. Science, or thought, which has material practice or being for its object, does not strive to reproduce nature in its integrity, in its entire perceptible substance, for these are already present. If science were to aim at nothing new, it would be superfluous. It is entitled to special recognition only to the extent that it carries a new element into matter. Science is not so much concerned in the material of its study as in understanding. Of course it is the understanding of this material which is desired, the understanding of its general character, of the fixed pole in the succession of phenomena. That which religion supernaturally separates from the material, which science opposes to the material as something higher, diviner, more spiritual, is in reality nothing but the faculty of rising above multiformity, of proceeding from the concrete to the general.

The nobler spiritual interests are not absolutely different from the material interests, they are not qualitatively different. The positive side of modern idealism does not consist in belittling eating and drinking, the pleasure in earthy possessions and in intercourse with the other sex, but rather in pleading for the recognition of other material enjoyments besides these, as for instance those of the eye, the ear, of art and science, in short of the whole man. You shall not indulge in the material revelries of passion, that is to say you shall not direct your thought one-sidedly to any concrete lust, but rather consider your entire development, take into account the total general extension of your existence. The bare materialist principle is inadequate in that it does not appreciate the difference between the concrete and the general, because it makes the individual synonymous with the general. It refuses to recognize the quantitative superiority of the mind over the world of sense perceptions. Idealism, on the other hand, forgets the qualitative unity in the quantitative difference. It is transcendental and makes an absolute difference out of the relative one. The contradiction between these two camps is due to the misunderstood relation of our reason to its given object or material. The idealist regards reason alone as the source of all understanding, while the materialist looks upon the world of sense perceptions in the same way. Nothing is required for a solution of this contradiction but the comprehension of the relative interdependence of these two sources of understanding. Idealism sees only the difference, materialism sees only the uniformity of matter and mind, content and form, force and substance, sense perception and moral interpretation. But all these distinctions belong to the one common genus which constitutes the distinction between the special and the general.

Consistent materialists act like purely practical men without any science. But, since knowing and thinking are real attributes of man regardless of his party affiliation, purely practical men do not exist in reality. Even the merest attempt at practical experiment on the basis of experienced facts differs only in degree from scientific practice based on theoretical principles. On the other hand, consistent idealists are just as impossible as purely practical men. They would like to have the general without the special, the spirit without matter, force without substance, science without experience or material, the absolute without the relative. How can thinkers who search for truth, being, relative causes, such as naturalists, be idealists? They are so only outside of their specialties, never inside them. The modern mind, the mind of natural science is immaterial only so far as it embraces all matters. But men like the astronomer Madler find so little of the ridiculous in the current expectation of the materially increased spiritual power after our "emancipation from the bonds of matter," that he has nothing better to substitute for it and flatters himself with having defined the "bonds of matter" as material attraction. Truly, so long as mind is still conceived in the form of a religious ghost, the expectation of an increased mental power after the emancipation from the bonds of matter is not so much an object for ridicule as for compassion. But if we regard mind as the expression of modern science, we offer the better scientific explanation for the traditional faith. By bond of matter we do not mean, in that case, the bond of gravitation, but the multiplicity of sense perception. And matter holds the mind in bondage only so long the faculty of thought has not overcome the multiplicity of things. The emancipation of the mind from the bonds of matter consists in developing the general element out of the concrete multiplicity.

(c) Force and Matter

The reader who has closely followed our main idea which will be further illustrated, will anticipate that the question of matter and force finds its solution in the understanding of the relation between the general and the special. What is the relation of the concrete to the abstract? This is the common problem of those who see the active impulse of the world either in the spiritual force or in the material substance, who think to find the nature of things, the non plus ultra of science, in either of these facts.

Liebig, who is especially fond of straying from his inductive science into the field of speculative thought, says in an idealist sense: "Force cannot be seen, we cannot grasp it with our hands; in order to understand its nature and peculiarities, we must investigate its effects." And if a materialist replies to him: "Matter is force, force is matter, no matter without force, no force without matter," it is plain that either has determined this relation only negatively. In certain shows, the clown is asked by the manager: "Clown, where have you been?" "With the others," answers the clown. "And where were the others?" "With me."

In this case we have two answers with the same content, in the other we have two camps which quarrel with different words about an indisputable fact. And this dispute is so much more ridiculous because it is taken so seriously. If the idealist makes a distinction between matter and force, he does not mean to deny that the real phenomenon of force is inseparably linked with matter. And if the materialist claims that there is no matter without force and no force without matter, he does not mean to deny that matter and force are different, as his opponent claims.

The dispute exists for a good reason and has its object, but this object is not revealed in the dispute is instinctively kept under cover by both parties so that they may not be in a position where they would have to acknowledge their own ignorance. Each wants to prove to the other that the other's explanations are inadequate, and both demonstrate this sufficiently. Buchner admits in the closing statement of his "Matter and Force" that the empirical material is insufficient to permit definite answers to transcendental questions, and that therefore no positive answer can be given to them. And he furthermore says that the empirical material "is fully sufficient to answer them negatively and to do away with hypothesis."

This is saying in so many words that the science of the materialist is adequate for the proof that his opponent knows nothing.

The spiritualist or idealist believes in a spiritual; which means in a ghostlike and inexplicable, nature force. The materialist thinkers, on the other hand are skeptical. A scientific proof of faith or of skepticism does not exist. The materialist has only this advantage over his idealist opponent, that he looks for the transcendental, the nature, the cause, the force, in back of the phenomenon, not outside of matter. But he remains behind the idealist when he ignores the difference between matter and force. The materialist dwells on the actual inseparability of matter and force and does not admit any other reason for a distinction between the two than "an external reason derives from the demand of our mind for systematization." Buchner says in "Nature and Mind," page 66: "Force and matter, separated from one another, are for me nothing but thoughts, fantasies, ideas without any substance, hypotheses which do not exist for any healthy study of nature, because all phenomena of nature are rendered obscure and unintelligible by such a separation." But if Buchner deals with any special department of natural science in a productive way, instead of handling phrases of natural philosophy; his own practice will show him that the separation of forces from matter is not an "external," but an internal, an imminent necessity, by which alone we are enabled to elucidate and understand the phenomena of nature. Although the author of "Force and Matter" chose for his motto: "Now, what I want is—facts," we assure the reader that this device is more a thoughtless word than a serious pinion. Materialism is not so coarse-grained that it wants purely facts. Those facts which Buchner is looking for are by themselves not specifics for his desires. The idealist likewise wants such facts. No student of nature wants mere hypotheses. What all cultivators of the field of science want is not so much facts as explanations or an understanding of facts. Even the materialist will not deny that science, the "natural philosophy" of Buchner not excepted, is more concerned with mental forces than with bodily matter, that it cares more for force than for matter. The separation of force and matter is derived from "the demand of our mind for systematization." Very true! But so does all science emanate from the demand of our reason for systematization.

The contradistinction between force and matter is as old as that between idealism and materialism. The first conciliation between the two was attempted by imagination, which, through the belief in spirits, suggested a secret nature as the cause of all natural phenomena. Science has of late expelled many of these special spirits by replacing the fantastic demons with scientific, or general, explanations. And after we have succeeded in explaining the demon of "pure" reason, it is not difficult to expel the special spirit of force by the general explanation of its nature and thus to reconcile scientifically the contradiction between spiritualism and materialism.

In the universe which constitutes the object of science and of the faculty of reason, both force and matter are unseparated. In the world of sense perceptions force is matter and matter is force. "Force cannot be seen." Oh, yes! Seeing itself is pure force. Seeing is as much an effect of its object as an effect of the eye, and this double effect and other effects are forces. We do not see the things themselves, but their effects on our eyes. We see their forces. And force cannot alone be seen, it can also be heard, smelled, tasted, felt. Who will deny that he can feel the force of heat, of cold, of gravitation? We have already quoted the words of Professor Koppe to the effect that we "cannot perceive heat itself, we merely conclude from its effects that this force exists in nature." This is saying in other words, that we do not see, hear, or feel the things themselves, but their effects or forces.

It is just as true to say that we feel matter and not its force as it is to say that we feel force and not matter. Indeed, both are inseparable from the object, as we have already remarked. But by means of the faculty of thought we separate from the simultaneously and successively occurring phenomena the general and the concrete. For instance, we abstract the general concept of sight from the various phenomena of our sight and distinguish it by the name of power of vision from the concrete objects, or substances, of our eyes. From a multitude of sense perceptions we develop by means of reason the general element. The general element of different water phenomena, for instance, is the water power distinguished from the substance of the water. If levers of different materials but of the same length have the same power, it is plain that in this case force is different from matter only in so far as it represents the general element of various substances. A horse does not pull without force, and this force does not pull without the horse. Indeed, in practice the horse is force and force is the horse. But nevertheless we may distinguish the power of pulling from other qualities of the horse, or we may refer to the common element in different services of horses as general horse power, without thereby starting from any other hypothesis than we do in distinguishing the sun from the earth. For in reality the sun does not exist without the earth, nor the earth without the sun.

The world of sense perceptions is made known to us only by our consciousness, but consciousness is conditioned on the world of sense perceptions. Nature is infinitely united or infinitely separated, according to whether we regard it from the standpoint of consciousness as an unconditional unit or from the standpoint of sense perceptions as an unconditional multiplicity. There is truth in both unity and multiplicity, but it is truth only relatively speaking, under certain conditions. It matters a great deal whether we look about with the eyes of the body or with the eyes of the mind. For the eyes of the mind, matter is force. For the eyes of the body, force is matter. The abstract matter is force, the concrete force is matter. Matter is represented by the objects of the hand, of practice, while force is an object of understanding, of science.

Science is not limited to the so-called scientific world. It reaches beyond all classes, it belongs to the full depth and width of life. Science belongs to thinking humanity in its entirety. And so it is with the separation of platter and force. Only a stultified fanaticism can ignore the practical distinction. The miser who accumulates money without adding any wealth to his life process forgets that the valuable element of money resides in its force, which is different from its substance. He forgets that not mere wealth as such, not the paltry gold substance, lends a reasonableness to the attest for its possession, but its spiritual content, its inherent exchange value, which buys the necessities of life. Every scientific practice, which means every action carried on with a predetermined success and with understood substances, proves that the separation of matter and force, though only performed in thought and existing in thought, is nevertheless not an empty phrase, not a mere hypothesis, but a very fertile idea. A farmer manuring his field is handling "pure" manuring force, in so far as it is immaterial for the abstract conception whether he is handling cow dung, bone dust, or guano. And in weighing bundles of merchandise, it is not the iron, copper, stone, etc., which is handled by the pound, but their gravity.

True, there is no force without matter, no matter without force. Forceless matter and matterless force are nonentities. If idealist naturalists believe in an immaterial existence of forces which, so to say, carry on their goblin-pranks in matter, forces which we cannot see, cannot perceive by the senses and yet are asked to believe in, then we say that such men are to that extent that naturists, but mere speculators, in other words spiritualists. And the word of the materialists who refer to the intellectual separation of matter and force as a mere hypothesis, is quite as brainless.

In order that this separation may be appreciated according to its merits, in order that our consciousness may neither etherealize force in a spiritualist sense nor deny it in a materialist sense, and in order to comprehend it scientifically, we have only to understand the faculty of thought in general or "in itself," that is to say its abstract form. The intellect can not operate without some perceptible material. In order to distinguish between matter and force, these things must exist and be experienced by sense perception. By means of this experience we refer to matter as the expression of force and to force as the expression of matter. The perceptible object which is to be studied is therefore matter and force in one, and since all objects are in their tangible reality such matter and force things, the distinction made by the mind consists in the general method of brain work, in the derivation of the general unity, from the special multiplicity in any one and in all given objects. The distinction between matter and force is summarized in the universal distinction between the concrete and the abstract. To deny the value of this distinction is equivalent to denying the value of any and all distinction, equivalent to ignoring the function of the intellect altogether. If we refer to phenomena of sense perception as forces of matter in general, then this generalized matter is nothing but an abstract conception. But if we mean by the term sense perception the various concrete substances, then the general element which embraces the differences of things and pervades and controls them is force producing concrete effects. And whether we say matter or force, the mental which science is studying, not with its hands, but with its brain, the so-called essence, nature, cause, ideal, superior or spiritual, is the generality comprising the special things.

V
"Practical Reason" or Morality

(a) The Wise and Reasonable

The understanding of the method of science, the understanding of the mind, is destined to solve all the problems of religion and philosophy, to explain thoroughly all the great and small riddles, and thus fully to restore research to its mission of empirically studying details. If we are aware that it is a law of reason to require some perceptible material, some cause, for its operation, then the question regarding the first or general cause becomes superfluous. Human understanding is then seen to be first and last cause of all concrete causes. If we understand that it is a law of reason to require for its operation some given object, some beginning at which to start, then the question of the first beginning must necessarily become inane. If we understand that reason derives abstract units out of concrete multiplicities, that it constructs truth out of phenomena, substance out of attributes, that it perceives all things as parts of a whole, as individuals of some genus, as qualities of some object, then the question regarding a "thing itself," a something which in reality is back of all things, must deeds become irrelevant. In brief, the understanding of the interdependence of reason reveals the unreasonableness of the demand for independent reason. Now, although the main object of metaphysics, the cause of all causes, the beginning of all beginnings, the nature of things, causes little inconvenience to modern science, and even though the needs of the present have overcome the leaning for speculation, this practical downfall of speculation does not suffice for the solution of its problems. So long as the theoretical law is not understood, according to which reason requires some concrete object for its operation, there is no hope of abandoning objectless thought, this malpractice of speculative philosophy, which pretends to generate knowledge without intercourse with objective reality. Our naturalists demonstrate this very clearly as soon as they turn from their tangible specialties to abstract things. The dispute over questions of life's wisdom, of morality, or the quarrel over the wise, good, right, or bad, reveals that here is the boundary of scientific agreement. The scientific explorers of the exact sciences abandon every day their inductive method when dealing with social problems, and stray off into the regions of speculative philosophy. Just as in physics they believe in imperceptible physical truths, in "things themselves," so in social matters they believe in the reasonable, wise, right, or bad, in the sense of "things themselves," of absolute phases of life, of unconditional conditions. It is here where the outcome of our studies, of the critique of pure reason, must be applied.

In recognizing that consciousness, the nature of understanding, the mental activity in its general form, consists in developing general concepts out of concrete objects, we circumscribe this insight by stating that reason develops its understanding out of contradictions. It is the nature of the mind to perceive, in given phenomena of different dimensions and different duration, the nature of things by their semblance, and their semblance by their nature; to distinguish in wants of various degrees the most essential and necessary from the less pressing; to measure within a certain circle of magnitudes the large by the small and the small by the large, or in other words to compare the contrasts of the world with one another, to harmonize them by explanation. Common parlance instinctively calls understanding judging; judging requires a certain standard. Just as surely as we cannot perceive any objects which are "in themselves" great or small, hard or soft, clear or dark, just as surely as these terms denote certain relations and require a certain standard by which their relations can be determined, even so does reason require a certain standard for the determination of that which is reasonable.

The fact that we consider certain actions, institutions, conceptions, maxims of other periods, nations, or persons unreasonable is simply due to the application of a different standard, because we ignore the premises, the conditions, which cause another's reason to differ from our own. Men who differ in their mental estimates, in their understanding of things, may be likened to the thermometers of Reaumur and Celsius, one of which designates the boiling point by 80 and the other by 100. A different standard is the cause of this different result. On the so-called moral field there is no scientific agreement, such as we enjoy in some physical matters, because we lack the uniform standard which natural science has long since found. It is still attempted to perceive the reasonable, good, right, etc., without empirical data, by speculative reasoning without experience. Speculation seek the cause of all causes, the immeasurable cause; troth "itself," the unconditional and standardless troth; the unlimited good, the unboundedly reasonable, etc. The absence of a standard is the essence of speculation, and its practice is characterized by unlimited inconsistency and disagreement. If there are followers of certain positive religions who agree in the matter of morals, they owe this to the positive standard which certain dogmas, doctrines and commandments have given them. But if any one tries to perceive things by "pure" reason, the dependence of this reason on some standard will be demonstrated by its "impure," that is to say individual, perceptions.

Sense perception is the standard of truth, or of science in general. The phenomena of the outside world are the standard of physical truths, and man with his many wants is the standard of moral truth. The actions of man are determined by his wants. Thirst teaches him to drink, need to pray. Wants are regulated in the South by southern conditions, in the North by northern conditions. Wants rule time and space, nations and individuals. They induce the savage to hunt and the gourmand to indulge. Human wants give to reason a standard for judging what is good, right, bad, reasonable, etc. Whatever satisfies our need is good, the opposite is bad. The physical feeling of man is the object of moral standards, the object of "practical reason." The contradictory variety of human needs is the basis for the contradictor: variety of moral standards. Because a member of feudal guilds prospered in a restricted competition and a modern knight of industry in free competition, because their interests differ, therefore their views differ, and the one justly considers an institution as unreasonable which the other regards as reasonable. If the intellect of some person attempts to define by mere introspection the standard of reasonableness as a general thing, this person makes himself or herself the standard of humanity. If reason is credited with the faculty of finding within itself the source of moral truth it commits the speculative mistake of attempting to produce understanding without perceptible objects. The same mistake is to blame for the idea that man is subordinate to the authority of reason, for the demand that man submit to the dictates of reason. This idea transforms man into an attribute of reason, while in reality reason is an attribute of man.

The question whether man depends on reason or reason on man is similar to the one whether the citizen exists for the state or the state for the citizen. In the last and highest instance, the citizen is the primary fact and the state is modified according to the requirements of the citizen. But whenever the dominant interests of the citizenship have acquired the authority in the state, then the citizen is indeed dependent an the state. This is saying in so many words that man is guided in minor matters by more important ones. He sacrifices the less important, minor, particular things to the great, essential, general things. He subordinates his desire for more individual indulgence to his fundamental social needs. It is not pure reason, but the reason of a weak body or of a limited purse which teaches man to renounce the pleasures of dissipation for the benefit of the general welfare. The wants of the senses are the material out of which reason fashions moral truths. To single out the essential need among different physical needs of various degrees of intensity or extension, to separate the true from the individual, to develop general concepts, that is the mission of reason. The difference between the apparently and the truly reasonable reduces itself to the difference between the special and the general.

We recall that reason requires sense perceptions for its existence and operation, that it needs some object which it can perceive. Existence is the condition or premise of all understanding. Just as the understanding of true existence is the function of natural science, so the understanding of reasonable existence is the function of wisdom. Reason in general has the mission of understanding things as they are. As physical science it has to understand what is true, as wisdom, what is reasonable. And just as true may be translated by general, so reasonable may be translated by generally appropriate to need. We saw a while ago that a sense perception is not true "in itself," but only relatively true, that it is called true or general only in relation to other perceptions of lesser importance. In the same way, no human action can be reasonable or appropriate "in itself," it can be reasonable only in comparison with some other action which attempts to accomplish the same purpose in a less practicable, that is an impracticable, form. Just as the true, the general, is conditioned on the relation to some other object, on a definite quantity of phenomena, on definite limits, so the reasonable or practicable is based on definite conditions which make it reasonable or unreasonable. The end in view is the measure of the practicable. The practicable can be determined only by some definite object that is wanted. Once this object is known, then that action is called reasonable which accomplishes it in the fullest, most general way, and all other actions appear unreasonable compared to it.

In view of the law which we evolved by our analysis of pure reason and which showed that all understanding, all thought, is based on some perceptible object, on some quantity of sense perceptions, it is evident that everything distinguished by our faculty of distinction is a certain quantity and that, therefore, all distinctions are only quantitative, not absolute, only graduated, not irreconcilable. Even the difference between the reasonable and the unreasonable, or in other words between that which is momentarily or individually reasonable and that which is generally reasonable, is merely a quantitative distinction, like all others, so that the unreasonable may be conditionally reasonable, and nothing is unreasonable but that which is supposed to be unconditionally reasonable.

If we understand that reason requires some perceptible object, some perceptible standard, then we shall no longer try to understand the absolutely reasonable, the purely reasonable. We shall then limit ourselves to look for the reasonable, as for all other things, in concrete objects. The definite, accurate, certain, uniform result of some understanding depends on the definite formulation of the task, on the accurate limitation of the perceptible quantity which is to be understood. If a certain moment, a certain person, certain class, a certain nation are given and at the same time an essential need, a general and predominating purpose, then the question regarding the reasonable or suitable is easily answered. It is true that we may also know something of things which are generally reasonable for mankind in the aggregate but in that case our standard must be abstract mankind instead of some concrete part of it. Science may study the anatomical structure of some concrete body as well as the general type of the human body, but this again it can do only when it supplies the faculty of understanding with general instead of individual material. If science divides the whole human race into four or five races, by establishing a certain standard of physiognomy, and later on discovers some individuals or tribes whose characters are so peculiar and rare that they cannot be classed under any of the established races, the existence of such exceptions is not a crime against the physical order of the world but merely a proof of the inadequacy of our scientific classification. If, on the other hand, some conventional mode of thought considers a certain action a universally reasonable or unreasonable and then encounters opposition in actual life, convention fancies itself exempt from the work of understanding and assumes to deny civic rights in the moral order of the world to its opponents. Instead of realizing the limited applicability of its rules by the existence of opposing practices, convention seeks to establish an absolute applicability of its rules by simply ignoring the cause of the opposition. This is a dogmatic procedure, a negative practice, which ignores facts on the pretense that they are irrational, but it is not a positive understanding, not an intelligent knowledge, such as manifests itself by the conciliation of contradictions.

If our study aims to ascertain what is universally human and reasonable, and if these predicates are given only to actions which are reasonable and practicable for all men, at all times, and under all conditions, then such concepts are absolute, indeterminate, and to that extent meaningless, indefinite generalities. We are stating such universal and indeterminate, and therefore unimportant and unpractical concepts, when we say that physically the whole is greater than a part, or that morally the good is preferable to the bad. The object of reason is that which is general, but it is the generality of some concrete object. The practice of reason deals with individual and concrete objects, with the things which are the opposite of the general, with special and concrete knowledge. In order to perceive in physics whether we are dealing with a part or with the whole object, we must handle definite and concrete objects or phenomena. If we desire to ascertain what is morally preferable as good or bad, we must start out with a definite quantity of human needs. Abstract and general reason, with its so-called eternal and absolute truths, is a phantasmagoria of ignorance which binds the rights of the individual with crushing chains. Real and true reason is individual, it cannot produce any other but individual perceptions, and these perceptions cannot be generalized to any greater extent than the general material with which they operate. Only that is universally reasonable which is acknowledged to be so by all reasons. If the reason of some time, class, or person is referred to as rational, and if some other time, clan or person considers it irrational; if, for instance, the Russian noble considers serfdom a rational institution and the English bourgeois the so-called liberty of his wage worker, both of these institutions are not absolutely rational, but only relatively, only in a more or less limited circle.

It is not necessary to state that I do not mean to question the great importance of our reason by the foregoing remarks. Even though reason cannot independently, or absolutely, discern the objects of the speculative introspection, such as the objects of the moral world, the true, the beautiful, the right, the bad the reasonable, etc., it nevertheless is well fitted to distinguish relatively, by means of concrete sense perceptions, between general and concrete things, between the object and its manifestation, between fundamental needs and fanciful appetites. Although we may dispense with the belief in absolute reason and consequently realize that there can be no absolute peace, still we may call war an unmitigated evil when comparing it with the peaceful interests of our time or of our class. Not until we abandon our fruitless exploring trip after absolute truth, shall we learn to find that which is true in space and time. It is precisely the consciousness of the relative applicability of our knowledge which is the strongest lever of progress. The believers in absolute truth have adopted the monotonous diagram of "good" men and "rational" institutions as a basis for their views of life. For this reason they oppose all human and historical institutions which do not fit into their pattern, but which reality nevertheless produces without regard to their brains. Absolute truth is the arch foundation of intolerance. On the other hand tolerance proceeds from the consciousness of the relative applicability of "eternal truths." The understanding of pure reason leads to the realization that the consciousness of the universal interdependence of reason is the true road toward practical reason.

(b) Morality and Right

The nature of our task limits us to the demonstration that pure reason is a nonentity, that reason is the sum of all acts of individual understanding, that it deals only seemingly with pure and general, but in reality with practical, or concrete, perceptions. We have been discussing that philosophy which pretends to be the science of pure or absolute understanding. We found its aim to be idle, inasmuch as the development of speculative philosophy represents a succession of disappointments, because its unconditional or absolute systems proved to be limited in space and time. Our presentation of the matter has revealed the relative character of so-called eternal truths. We perceived that reason was dependent on sense perceptions, we found that any truth required definite limits for its determination. As regards more especially life's wisdom, we saw that the acquired knowledge of "pure" reason manifested itself in practice by the dependence of the wise or the rational upon concrete sense perceptions. If we now apply this theory to morality as such, we must be able to establish harmony also in this field, where there is some doubt as to what is right and wrong, by means of the scientific method.

Pagan morality is different from Christian morality. Feudal morality differs from modern bourgeois morality as does bravery from solvency. In brief, we need no detailed illustration to show that different times and nations have different moralities. We have but to understand that this change is a necessary, special characteristic of the human race and of historical development, and we shall then exchange the belief in "eternal truths," which every ruling class claims to be identical with its own selfish laws, for the scientific knowledge that absolute right is purly a concept which we derive by means of the faculty of thought from the various successive rights. Right as an absolute concept means no more and no less than any other general concept, for instance, the head in general. Every real head is a concrete one and belongs either to man or to some other animal, it is either long or broad, narrow or wide, in other words it has special peculiarities. But at the same time every concrete head has certain general qualities which are universal in all heads, for instance the qualities of being the superintendent of the body. More over, every head has as many general as individual traits, it is no more personal than it is common. The faculty of thought abstracts the general traits from the actual concrete heads and in this way creates the concept of the absolute head. Just as the absolute head or *the* head, is composed of the general qualities all heads, so the absolute right stands merely for the general characters of all rights. Both of these concepts exist merely as ideas, not as objects.

Every real right is a concrete right, it is right only under certain conditions, at definite periods, for this or that nation. "Thou shalt not kill," is right in peace, but wrong in war; it is right for the majority of bourgeois society that wishes to see the outbursts of passion controlled in the interest of its own predominant needs, but wrong for the savage who has not arrived at the period where a peaceful and social life is appreciated, and who therefore would consider the above commandment as an immoral restriction of his liberty. For the love of life, murder is a detestable abomination, for revenge it is a sweet satisfaction. In the same way robbery seems right to the robber, wrong to the robbed. There can be no question of any absolute wrong in such cases, only of wrong in a relative sense. An action is wrong in a general sense only in so far as it is generally disliked. Plain robbery is wrong in the opinion of the great majority today because our generation takes more interest in bourgeois affairs of commerce and industry than in the adventures of the knights of the road.

If there were such a thing as an absolutely right law, dogma, or action, it would have to serve the welfare of all mankind under all conditions and at all times. But human welfare is as different as men, circumstances, and time. What is good for me is bad for another, and the thing which may be beneficial as a rule may be injurious as an exception. What promotes some interests in one period may interfere with them in another. A law which would presume to be absolutely right would have to be right for every one and at all times. No absolute morality, no duty, no categorical imperative, no idea of the good can teach man what is good, bad, right, or wrong. That is good which corresponds to our needs, that is bad which is contrary to them. But is there anything which is absolutely good? Everything and nothing. It is not the straight timber which is good, nor the crooked. Neither is good, or either is good, according to whether I need it or not. And since we need all things, we can see some good in all of them. We are not limited to any one thing. We are unlimited, universal, and need everything. Our interests are therefore innumerable, inexpressibly great, and therefore every law is inadequate, because it always considers only some special welfare, some special interest. And for this reason no right is right, or all of them are right, and it is as right to say "Thou shalt not kill" as it is to say "Thou shalt kill."

The difference between good needs and bad needs, right wants and wrong wants, like that between truth and error, reasonable and unreasonable, finds its conciliation in the difference between the concrete and the general. Reason cannot discover within itself any positive rights or absolutely moral codes any more than any other speculative truth. It cannot estimate how essential or unessential a thing is, or classify the quantity of concrete and general characters, until it has some perceptible material to work upon. The understanding of the right, or of the moral, like all understanding, strives to single out the general characteristics of its object. But the general is only possible within certain defined limits, it exists only as the general qualities of some concrete and determined perceptible object. And if any one tries to represent some maxim, some law, some right in the light of an absolute maxim, law or right, he forgets this necessary limitation. Absolute right is merely a meaningless concept, and it does not assume even a vague meaning until it is understood to stand for the right of mankind in general. But morality, or the determination of that which is right, has a practical purpose. Yet, if we accept the general and unconditional right of mankind as a moral right, we necessarily miss our practical aim. An act or a line of action which is universally or everywhere right requires no law for its enforcement, for it will recommend itself. It is only the determined and limited law, adapted to certain persons, classes, nations, times, or circumstances, which has any practical value, and it is so much more practical the more defined, exact, precise and the less general it is.

The most universal and most widely recognized right or need is in its quality no more rightful, better, or valuable than the most insignificant right of the moment, than the momentary need of some individual. Although we know that the sun is hundreds of thousands of miles in diameter, we are nevertheless free to see it no larger than a plate. And though we may acknowledge that some moral law is theoretically or universally good or holy, we are free in practice to reject it momentarily, in parts, or individually, as bad and useless. Even the most sacred right of the most universal extent is valid only within certain definite limits, and within particular limits an otherwise very great wrong may be a valid right. It is true that there is an eternal difference between assumed and true interests, between passion and reason, between essential, predominating, general, well-founded needs and inclinations, and accidental, subordinate, special appetites. But this difference is not one of two separated worlds, a world of the good and a world of the bad. It is not a positive, general, continuous, absolute difference, but merely a relative one. Like the difference between beautiful and homely, it depends on the individuality of the person who distinguishes. That which is a true and fundamental need in one case, is a secondary, subordinate, and wrong desire in another.

Morality is the aggregate of the most contradictory ethical laws which serve the common purpose of regulating the conduct of man toward himself and others in such a way that the future is considered as well as the present, the one as well as the other, the individual as well as the genus. The individual man finds himself lacking, inadequate, limited in many ways. He requires for his complement other people, society, and must therefore live and let live. The mutual concessions which arise out of these relative needs are called morality.

The inadequacy of the single individual, the need of association, is the basis and cause of man's consideration for his neighbor, of morality. Now since the one who feels this need, man, is necessarily an individual, it follows that his need must likewise be individual and more or less intensive. And since my neighbors are necessarily different from me, it requires different considerations to meet their needs. Concrete man needs a concrete morality. Just as abstract and meaningless as the concept of mankind in general is that of absolute morality, and the ethical laws derived from this vague idea are quite as unpractical and unsuccessful. Man is a living personality, whose welfare and purpose is embodied within himself, who has between himself and the world nothing but his needs as a mediator, who owes no allegiance to any law whatever from the moment that it contravenes his needs. The moral duty of an individual never exceeds his interests. The only thing which exceeds those interests is the *material power* of the generality over the individuality.

If we regard it as the function of reason to ascertain that which is morally right, a uniform scientific result may be produced if we agree at the outset on the persons, conditions, or limits within which the universal moral right is to be determined; in other words, we may accomplish something practical if we drop the idea of absolute right and search for definite rights applicable to well-defined purposes by clearly stating our problem. The contradiction in the various standards of morality, and the many opposing solutions of this contradiction, are due to a misunderstanding of the problem. To look for right without a given quantity of sense perceptions, without some definite working material, is an act of speculative reason which pretends to explore nature without the use of senses. The attempt to arrive at a positive determination of morality by pure perception and pure reason is a manifestation of the philosophical faith in understanding *a priori*.

"It is true," said Macaulay in his History of England, in speaking of the rebellion against the lawless and cruel government of James II., "that to trace the exact boundary between rightful and wrongful resistance is impossible; but this impossibility arises from the nature of right and wrong, and is found in every part of ethical science. A good action is not distinguished from a bad action by marks so plain; those which distinguish a hexagon from a square. There is a frontier where virtue and vice fade in each other. Who has ever been able to define the exact boundary between courage and rashness, between prudence and cowardice, between frugality and avarice, between liberality and prodigality? Who has ever been able to say how far mercy to offenders ought to be carried, and where it ceases to deserve the name of mercy and becomes pernicious weakness?"

It is not the impossibility of accurately determining this limit to which the nature of the difference between right and wrong, in the sense of Macaulay, is due. It is rather due to the vague thought which believes in an unlimited right, in absolute virtues and faults, which has not risen to the understanding that; the terms good, brave, right, and bad are valid always and everywhere only in relation to some concrete individual who reasons, and that they have no validity in themselves. Courage is foolhardiness in the eye of the cautious, and caution is cowardice in the opinion of the daring. The revolt against existing governments is always right in the eyes of the rebels, always wrong in the opinion of the attacked. No action can be absolutely right or wrong.

The same qualities of man are good or bad, according to his needs and their uses, according to time and place. Here trickery, slyness, and bad faith prevail, there loyalty, frankness and straightforwardness. Here compassion and charity serve their purpose and promote welfare, there ruthless and bloody severity. The quantity, the more or less beneficial effect of a human quality, determines the difference between virtue and vice.

Reason can distinguish between right and wrong, virtue and vice, only to the extent that it can measure the relative quantity of right in any faculty, rule, or action. No categorical imperative, no ethical code, can serve as a basis for the real practical right. On the contrary, ethics finds its justification in the actual righteousness of perceptible objects. For general reason, frankness is not a better quality than slyness. Frankness is preferable to slyness only inasmuch as it is quantitatively, that is to say, more frequently, better, and more generally appreciated than slyness. It follows that a science of right can serve as a guide in practice only to the extent that practice has served as a basis for science. Reason cannot determine the action of man beforehand, because it can only experience, but not anticipate reality, because every man, every situation, is new, original, exists for the first time, and because the possibilities of reason are confined to understanding *a posteriori*.

Absolute right, or right in itself, is an imagined right, is a speculative desire. A scientifically universal right requires certain definite and perceptible premises which form the basis of the determination of the general. Science is not a dogmatic infallibility which may say: This or that is right, because it is so understood. Science requires for its perceptions some external object. It can perceive right only if it rightly exists. The universal existence is the material, premise, condition, and cause of science.

From the foregoing follows the postulate that morality must be studied inductively or scientifically, not speculatively by the method of traditional philosophy. We must not attempt to study absolute, but only relative rights, only rights based on certain premises, and only this can be the moral problem of reason. Thus the belief in a moral order of the world is dissolved in the consciousness of human freedom. The understanding of reason, of knowledge, of science, includes the understanding of the limited validity of all ethical maxims.

Whatever impressed man as salutary, valuable, divine, was exhibited by him in the tabernacle of faith as the most venerable thing. The Egyptian worshiped the cat, the Christian venerates the divine providence. So, when his needs led him to live a well-regulated life, the benefits of the law inspired him with such a high opinion of its noble origin that he adopted his own handiwork as a gift of heaven. The invention of the mouse-trap or other useful appliances pushed the cat out of its exalted position. Whenever man becomes his own master, takes care of himself, and provides for himself, then all other providences become useless, and his own mastership makes all superior tutelage unbearable. Man is a jealous creature. Ruthlessly he subordinates everything to his own interests, even God and His commandments. No matter how great or venerable an authority any code may have acquired by long and faithful service, as soon as new needs oppose it, they degrade the divine authority to the ranks of human law and transform ancient right into modern wrong. The Christian frivolity refused to respect the threat of physical retribution which the Hebrew had anointed as an authority in moral questions and revered under the maxim: Eye for eye, tooth for tooth. The Christian had learned to cherish the blessings of peacefulness; he carried submissive tolerance into the holy land, and decorated the vacant tabernacle with the gentle injunction to offer the left cheek when the right was tired of cuffs. In our times which are Christian in name, but very anti-Christian in deeds, the long venerated tolerance has long gone out of use.

Just as every religion has its own peculiar God, so every time has its own peculiar right. To this extent, religion and morality are in harmony with the worship of their sanctum. But they become arrogant upstarts whenever they assume to exceed their natural boundaries, whenever they attempt to saddle upon all circumstances, under the pretense of offering something incomparable, absolute, permanent, that which is divine and right at certain times and under definite conditions; whenever they proclaim a successful remedy for their own peculiar disease as a universal patent medicine for all diseases; whenever they overbearingly forget their descent. A law is originally dictated by some individual need, and then mankind with its universal needs is supposed to balance itself on the thin rope of this one rule. Originally that which is really good is right, and thereafter only some decreed right is supposed to be really good. That is the unbearable arrogance. Ordained right is not satisfied to serve as the right of this time, this nation or country, this class or caste. It wants to dominate the whole world, wants to be absolute right, just as if a certain pill could be absolute medicine, could be good for everything. It is the mission of progress to repulse this assumption, to pluck this peacock feather out of the tail of the rooster, by leading mankind on beyond the boundaries prescribed by ordained law, extending the world for him, by conquering for his cramped interests a wider liberty. The migration from Palestine to Europe where the consumption of pork does not cause leprosy emancipates our natural freedom from a once divine restriction by making it irrelevant. But progress does not deprive one God of his shoulder straps for the purpose of decorating some other God with them.

That would merely be an exchange, not an acquirement. Evolution does not drive the saints of tradition out of the country; it simply retires them from the wrongfully occupied field of universality into their peculiar boundaries. Progress picks up the child and then pours the water out of the bath tub. Through the cat may have lost its aureole and ceased to be a God, it does not give up catching mice; and though the Jewish rules for bodily cleanliness at certain definite times have long been forgotten, a clean body is still highly respected. The present wealth of civilization is due only to the economical administration of the acquirements of the past. Evolution is as much conservative as it is revolutionary, and it finds as much wrong as right in every law.

It is true that the believers in absolute duty scent a difference between moral and legal right. But their self-interested narrowness does not permit them to realize that every law is originally moral and that every special morality is gradually reduced to the level of a mere law. Their understanding reaches into other times and other classes, but does not reach their own time and class. The laws of the Chinese and Samoyeds are understood to refer to the peculiar requirements of those people. But the rules of bourgeois society are supposed to be far more sublime. Our present day institutions and moral codes are either regarded as eternal truths of nature or reason, or as permanent oracular expressions of a pure conscience. Just as if the barbarian did not have a barbarian reason; as if the Turk did not have a Turkish conscience and the Hebrew a Hebrew one; as if man could follow the dictates of some absolute conscience, instead of the conscience being conditioned on the man.

Whoever limits the purpose of man to the love and service of God, and to eternal blessedness hereafter, may devoutly recognize the traditions of abstract morality as authoritative and guide himself accordingly. But whoever regards development, education, and blessedness on earth as man's life purpose, will not think that the questioning of the assumed superiority of traditional morals is irrelevant. It is only the consciousness of individual freedom which creates sufficient unconcern for the rules made by others to permit a brave advance, which emancipates us from the striving for an illusory absolute ideal, for some "best world," and which restores us to the definite practical interests of our time and personality. At the same time we are thus reconciled with the world as it really is, because we no longer regard it as the unsuccessful realization of that which ought to be, but rather as the systematization of that which cannot but be. The world is always right. Whatever exists, is right and is not fated to be otherwise until it changes. Wherever there is existence, which is power, there is also right without any further condition, because it is right in a formative stage. Weakness has no other right than that of striving for supremacy and then enforcing a recognition of its long denied needs. The study of history shows us not only the negative and ridiculous side of the religions, customs, institutions and ideas of the past, but also their positive, reasonable and necessary side. It explains to us, for instance, that the deification of animals was due to an enthusiastic recognition of their usefulness. And so the study of history shows not alone the inadequacy of the things of the present, but also demonstrates that they are the reasonable and necessary conclusions from the premises of previous stages.

(c) The Holy

In the well-known statement: The end sanctifies the means, the developed theory of morality finds its practical expression. This maxim, used in an ambiguous sense, may stand as a common reproach for us and for the Jesuits. The defenders of the society of Jesus make efforts to prove that it is a malignant attempt to discredit their clients. We shall not try to speak for either party to this dispute, but will devote ourselves to the subject matter itself, and seek to substantiate the truth and reasonableness of this maxim, to rehabilitate it in the public opinion.

It will be sufficient for the refutation of the most general opposition to understand that end and means are very relative terms, that all concrete ends are means and all means are ends. There is no more of a positive difference between great and small, right and wrong, virtue and vice, than there is between end and means. Considered as something integral by itself, every action has its own end and its means are the various moments of which even the shortest action is composed. Every concrete action is a means in relation to other actions which aim at the same common effect. But in themselves actions are neither ends nor means. Nothing is anything by itself. All being is relative. Things are what they are only within and by their interrelations. Circumstances alter cases.

In so far as every action is accompanied by other actions, it is a means, and serves a common end which exceeds its own special end; but inasmuch as every action is complete in itself it is an end which includes its own means. We eat in order to live; but so far as we are living while we are eating, we are living in order to eat. As life to its functions, so the end is related to its means. Just as life is simply the sum of all life's functions, so the end is the sum of all its means. The difference between means and end reduces itself to that between the concrete and the general. And all abstract differences reduce themselves to this difference, because the faculty of abstraction or distinction reduces itself to the faculty of distinguishing between the concrete and the general. But this distinction presupposes the existence of some material, some given objects, some circle of sense perceptions by which it manifests itself. If this circle is found in the field of actions or functions, in other words, if a previously defined number of different actions is the object of our study, then we refer to the general character of these objects as the general end and to every more or less extended part of them, or to every function, as a means. Whether any definite action is considered as an end or as a means, depends on the question whether we consider it as a whole in relation to its own parts, or as a part of some whole in which it is connected with other parts, with other actions. From a general point of view which has all human actions for the object of its study, and encompasses them all, there exists only one end, viz., the human welfare. This welfare is the end of all ends, is the final end, is the real, true, universal end compared to which all special ends are but means.

Now, our claim that the end sanctifies the means can have absolute validity only in regard to some absolute end. But all concrete ends are relative and finite. The one and sole absolute end is human welfare, and it is an end which sanctifies all rules and actions, all means, so long as they are subservient to it, but which reviles them as soon as they go their own way without serving it. The human weal is literally and historically the origin of the holy. That which is hale is holy. At the same time we must not ignore the fact that the weal, or hale, in general, the hale which sanctifies all means, is but an abstraction, the real content of which is as different as are the times, the nations, or persons which are seeking for their welfare. It must be remembered that the determination of that which is holy or for the human weal requires definite conditions, that no action, no means, is holy in itself, that each one of them is sanctified only by definite relations. It is not every end which sanctifies the means, but the holy end which sanctifies its own means. But since every real and concrete end is only relatively holy, it can sanctify its own means only relatively.

The opposition against our maxim is not so much directed against it, as against the wrong application of it.

Recognition is denied and the so-called sanctified ends are accorded only limited means, because there is lurking in the background the consciousness that these ends have only a relative holiness. On the other hand our defense of the maxim does not imply that the various nominally holy means and ends are sanctified because some authority, some scriptural statement, some reason or conscience, has declared them to be so, but only in so far as they answer the common end of all ends, the human welfare. Our maxim of ends does not at all teach that we should sacrifice love and truths to sanctified faith, but neither does it demand that we should sacrifice faith for love and truth. It merely states the fact that, whenever some superior end has been determined by sense perceptions or circumstances, all means contrary to that end are unholy, and that on the other hand means which are generally unholy may become temporarily and individually sanctioned by their relation to some momentary or individual welfare. Wherever peacefulness is actually in favor as a sanctified means, war is unholy. When, on the other hand, man seeks his salvation in war, then murder and incendiarism are holy means. In other words, our reason requires for a valid determination of that which is sanctified certain definite material conditions or facts as premises; it cannot determine the holy in general, not *a priori*, not philosophically in the old speculative way, but only in concrete cases, *a posteriori*, only empirically.

If we understand that human welfare is the end of all ends, the ideal of all means; if we furthermore dispense with all special determinations of this welfare, with all personal ideas of it, and recognize that it is different under different circumstances, then we understand at the same time that no means is sanctified beyond the sanctity of its end. No means, no action, is positively sanctified or makes for human welfare under all circumstances. According to circumstances and relations one and the same means may be good or bad. A thing is good only to the extent that its results are good, only to the extent that there is good in its end. Lying and cheating are bad only because they result injuriously for ourselves, because we do not wish to be lied to or cheated. But whenever a sanctified end is in question, the deceptive means used in lying and cheating are called tricks of war. If any one is firmly rooted in the goodness of chastity because he thinks it was ordained by God, we cannot discuss the matter with him. But if one honors virtue for the sake of virtue and abhors vice for the sake of vice, in other words, for their consequences, he admits that he sacrifices the lust of the flesh to the end of good health. In short, he admits that the means are sanctified by the end.

In the Christian conception of the world, the commandments of its religion are absolutely good for all time, they are considered good because Christian revelation declares them to be so. This conception does not know that, for instance, its acme of virtue, the specifically Christian virtue of abstemiousness, received its value only by contrast with corrupt heathenish licentiousness, but that it is not a virtue when compared to reasonable and normal satisfaction of material needs. It deals with certain means which it calls indiscriminately good without any relation to their ends, and others which it calls indiscriminately bad in the same absolute way. And for this reason, it opposes the above named maxim.

But modern Christianity, modern civilization, has practically long done away with this faith. It does indeed call the soul the likeness of God and the body a putrid food for worms; but its deeds prove that it does not take its religious phrases seriously. It cares little for the better part of man and directs all its thoughts and actions toward the satisfaction of the despised body. It employs science and art, and the products of all climates, for the glorification of the body, clothing it sumptuously, feeding it luxuriously, caring for it tenderly, resting it on soft cushions. Although they speak slightingly of this earthly life in comparison to the eternal life beyond, yet in practice they cling for six days of the week to the uninterrupted pleasures of this body, while heaven is hardly considered worthy of careless attention for more than one short hour on Sundays. With the same thoughtless inconsistency the so-called Christian world also attacks our maxim with words, while in practical life it sanctifies the despised means by the end of its own welfare, going even so far as to demonstrate its inconsistency in its own life by subsidizing prostitution with state funds. The fact that the legislative bodies of our representative states keep down the enemies of their bourgeois order by court-martials and exile, that they justify this course by the proverb, "Do unto others as you would that they should do unto you," in the interest of "public" welfare, or that they defend their divorce codes by the plea of individual welfare, proves that the bourgeoisie also believes in the motto the end sanctifies the means. And even though the citizens delegate rights to the state which they deny to themselves, also our opponents cannot but admit that in so doing the citizens are simply delegating their own rights to the superior authority of the state.

True, whoever employs lying and cheating in the bourgeois world for the end of gaining wealth, even though he may make it one of his ends to give to charity, or whoever steals leather, like Saint Chispinus, for the purpose of making shoes for poor people, does not sanctify his means by his end, because the end in that case is not sanctified, or only nominally so, only in general, but not in the concrete case quoted. For charity is an end of but inferior holiness which must not be more than a means compared to the main end of maintaining bourgeois society, and whenever it contravenes this main purpose, charity loses its character of a good end. And we have already seen that an end which is sanctified only under certain circumstances cannot sanctify its means beyond them. The indispensable condition of all good ends is that they must be subservient to human welfare, and whether this welfare is secured by Christian or pagan, by feudal or bourgeois means, it always demands that the things which are considered unessential and of lesser importance should be subordinated to the essential and necessary things, while in the above quoted cases the more salutary honesty and bourgeois respectability would be sacrificed to the less salutary charity. "The end sanctifies the means" signifies in other words that in ethics as well as in economics, the profit must justify the investment of the capital. Again, if we call the forcible conversion of infidels a good end, and an arbitrary police measure a bad means, this does not prove anything against the truth of the maxim, but only testifies to its wrong application. The means is not sanctified in the case, because the end is not, because a forced conversion is not a good end, but rather an evil one resulting in hypocrisy, and because such a conversion does not deserve this name, or because force is a means which is unworthy of this term. If it is true that a forcible conversion or wooden iron are senseless ideas, how is it that people will persist in fighting against universally recognized truths with such inconsistencies, such inane word plays, such tricks of rhetoric and sophistry? The means of the Jesuits, sly tricks and intrigues, poison and murder, appear unholy to us only because the Jesuitic purpose, for instance that of extending the wealth and influence and glorifying power of the order, is an inferior end which may make use of the innocent language of the pulpit, but is not an absolutely sanctified end, no supreme end, to which we would grant means that would deprive us of some essential end, for instance of our personal and public safety. Murder and manslaughter are considered immoral as individual actions because they are not means to accomplish our main end, because we incline not toward revenge or bloodthirstiness, nor toward arbitrariness and the willful dispensation of justice by some judge, but toward lawful decisions and the more or less impartial decrees of the state. But do we not explicitly declare in favor of the maxim "The end sanctifies the means," when we constitute ourselves into juries and render dangerous criminals powerless by the rope and the ax of the executioner?

The same people who boast of having dropped Aristotle, that is to say the belief in authority, for centuries, and who therefore replaced the dead traditional truth by living self-gained truth, are found to be completely at odds with their own development in the above cited cases. If we listen to the recital of some funny story, which may be told by even a reliable witness, we nevertheless remain loyal to the principles of free reason, that is to say we are free to regard as serious and regrettable any incident which the narrator may consider funny and ridiculous. People know how to distinguish between a story and the subjective impression its incidents created on the mind of the narrator, and which depends more on the personality of the witness than on the actual facts. But in the matter of good ends and bad means it is proposed to neglect the distinction between an object and its subjective end which is otherwise the point of all critique. Such ends as charity, the conversion of infidels, etc., are thoughtlessly, *a priori*, called good and holy, because they once were so under particular conditions, while now their effect in the cases above cited is just the opposite, and then people wonder that the unrighteous title carries with it unrighteous privileges.

Only that end is worthy of the predicate good or holy in practice which is itself a means, a servant, of the end of all purposes, of welfare. Whenever man seeks his welfare in bourgeois life, in production and commerce of commodities, and in the undisturbed enjoyment of his private property, he clips his long fingers by the commandment "Thou shalt not steal." But wherever, as among the Spartans, war is regarded as the supreme end and craftiness as a necessary quality of a warrior, there thieving is used as a means of acquiring craftiness and sanctioned as a means for the main end. To blame the Spartan for being a warrior instead of a sedate bourgeois would be to ignore the facts of reality, would be equivalent to overlooking that our brain is not designed to substitute imaginary pictures for the actual conditions of the world, but is organized to understand that a period, a nation, an individual is always that which it can and must be under given circumstances.

It is not from mere individual and unpraiseworthy fondness for the paradox that we subvert current views by defending the maxim "The end sanctifies the means," but from a consistent application of the science of philosophy. Philosophy originated out of the belief in a dualist contrast between God and the world, between body and soul, between the flesh and the spirit, between brain and senses, between thinking and being, between the general and the concrete. The conciliation of this contrast represents the end, or the aggregate result, of philosophical research. Philosophy found its dissolution in the understanding that the divine is worldly and the worldly divine, that the soul is related to the body, the spirit to the flesh, thinking to being, the intellect to the senses, in the same way in which the unity is related to the multiplicity or the general to the concrete. Philosophy began with the erroneous supposition that the one, as the first thing, was the basis on which developed the two, three, four, and the entire multiplicity of things by succession. It has now arrived at the understanding that truth, or reality, turns this supposition upside down, that the reality with its multiplicity of forms, perceivable by the senses, is the first and foremost thing out of which the human brain gradually derived the conception of unity or generality.

No achievement of science can be compared with the amount of talent and intellectual energy consumed in harvesting this one little fruit from the field of speculative philosophy. But neither does any scientific novelty encounter so many deep-rooted obstacles to its recognition. All brains unfamiliar with the outcome of philosophy are dominated by the old belief in the reality of some genuine, true, absolutely universal panacea, the discovery of which would make all sham, false individual panaceas impossible. But we, on the other hand, have been taught by the understanding of the thought process that this coveted panacea is a product of the brain and that, since it is supposed to be a general and abstract panacea, it cannot be any real, perceptible, concrete panacea. In the belief in an absolute difference between true and false welfare, there is manifested an ignorance of the actual operations of brain work. Pythagoras made numbers the basis of things. If this Grecian philosopher could have realized that this basic nature was a thing of the mind, of the intellect, and that numbers were the basis of reason, the common or abstract content of all intellectual activity, then we should have been spared all the disputes which have raged around the various forms of absolute truth, about "things in themselves."

Space and time are the general forms of reality, or reality exists in time and space. Consequently all real welfare must be attached to space and time, and every welfare which exists in these dimensions must be real. The different welfares, in so far as their beneficent qualities are concerned, are to be distinguished only by their height and breadth, by the quantity of their dimensions, by their numeral relations. Every welfare, whether true or seeming, is perceived by the senses, by practices of life, not by abstract reason. But practice assigns the most contradictory things to different people at different times as means to their welfare. What is welfare in one place, is disaster in another, and vice versa. Understanding, or reason, has nothing else to do in the matter than to number these various welfares as they are made real by sense perceptions in various persons and times, and degrees of intensity, in the order in which they appear, and thus to distinguish the small from the great, the essential from the unessential, the concrete from the general. Reason cannot dictate to us autocratically in matters of some absolutely true welfare, it can only indicate the most frequent, most essential, and most universal welfare in a certain perceived number of welfares. But it must not be forgotten that the truth of such an understanding, or enumeration, depends on certain definite premises. It is therefore a vain endeavor to search for the true and absolute welfare. This search becomes practical and successful only when it limits itself to the understanding of a definite amount of welfare of some particular objects. The general welfare can be found only within definite boundaries. But the various determinations of welfare agree in this respect, that they all consider it well to sacrifice the little for the great, the unessential for the essential, and not vice versa. In so far as this principle is right, it is also right for us to employ for the good end of a great welfare some small means in the shape of a small evil and to endure it, and thus we see once more that the end sanctifies the means.

If people were liberal enough to permit every one to go to heaven in his or her own way, the opponents of our maxim would be easily convinced of its truth. But instead of doing this, people follow the usual course of shortsightedness and make their private standpoint a universal one. They call their own private welfare the only true welfare, and regard the welfare of other nations, times and conditions a mistake. So does every school of art declare its own subjective taste to be objective beauty, ignoring the fact that unity is but a matter of ideas, of thought, while reality is full of the most varied forms. The real welfare is manifold

and urges us to renounce the superfluous in order to secure and retain the necessary. Thus your duty is your self-interest and your self-interest your duty.

If our ideas are to adapt themselves to truth, or to reality, instead of reality or truth adapting itself to our notions or thoughts, we must understand that the mutability of that which is right, holy, moral, is a natural, necessary and true fact. And we must grant to an individual the theoretical freedom which cannot be taken from it in practice, we must admit that it is as free now as it has ever been, that laws must be adapted to the needs of the social individual and not to the vague, unreal, and impossible abstractions, such as justice or morality. What is justice? The embodiment of all that is considered right, an individual conception, which assumes different forms in different persons. In reality only individual, definite, concrete rights exist, and man simply comes along and abstracts from them the idea of justice, just as he abstracted from different kinds of wood the conception of wood in general, or from material things the conception of matter. It is just as far from the truth, to think that material things consist of, or are by virtue of, abstract matter, although this view is widely spread, as it is to believe that the moral or bourgeois laws were derived from the idea of justice.

The ethical loss caused by our realistic, or if you prefer, materialistic, conception of morality is not so great as it appears. We need not fear that through this conception social beings will become lawless cannibals or hermits. Freedom and lawfulness are closely allied by the need for association which compels us to permit others to live together with us. If a man is prevented by his conscience or by other spiritualistic or bourgeois ethics from committing unlawful actions—unlawful in the wider meaning of the term—he is either not exposed to very grave temptations, or he has a nature so tame that the natural or legal punishments fully suffice to keep him within prescribed bounds. But where these checks are ineffective, morality is likewise powerless. If it were otherwise, we should have to assume that morality exerts in secret the same influence on the faithful which is exerted by public opinion on the faithless. But we know from actual experience that there are more pious thieves than infidel robbers. That the world, which attributes so much value for social welfare to morality by word of mouth, actually shares this view of ours, is proven by the fact that bourgeois society gives more attention to the penal code and to the police than to the influence of morality.

Moreover, our fight is not directed against morality, not even against any special form of it, but only against the arrogance which assumes to stamp some concrete form of morality with the trade mark of absolute morality. We recognize that morality is eternally sacred, in so far as it refers to considerations which a man owes to himself and to his fellowmen in the interest of their common welfare. But the freedom of the individual demands that each one should be at liberty to determine the degree of consideration and the manner of giving it expression. Under these circumstances it is as inevitable that the ruling powers, classes or majorities should enforce their special needs under the form of a prescribed right, as it is that a man's shirt should be closer to his skin than his coat. But it appears to us not merely very superfluous, but even detrimental to the energies required for the progress of the future, that some decreed right should be elevated to the position of absolute right and transformed into an insuperable barrier to the advance of humanity.

A Dietzgen Biography

by Larry Gambone

Dietzgen was born near Cologne in 1828 and in his youth apprenticed as a tanner, which became his lifelong occupation. He participated in the Revolution of 1848 and at that time first read the writings of Karl Marx and became one of his supporters. Marx had a high regard for this man known as "the Tanner", considering him one of the few people to understand his ideas, even going so far as to mention this in his introduction to *Capital*. Dietzgen was a frequent contributor to Social Democratic newspapers, particularly the *Volkstaat*, but it was not until 1869 that his first book, *The Nature of Human Brain Work*, was published.

Fleeing Germany a year after the failed revolution, the young Dietzgen went to the United States, where he stayed for two years, spending most of his time traveling and observing American life. He returned to Germany and revisited the US in 1859, this time staying for three years. On returning home, he got a position managing a tannery in Russia, for he was excellent at his craft.

Back in Germany again after the Russian sojourn, he ran for parliament under the banner of the Social

Democratic Party, but was not elected. In 1878, Dietzgen spent a year in prison for writing a radical pamphlet. In spite of this ordeal, he kept his characteristic humility and sense of humor, declaring after release, "I was handcuffed to another rascal." (Note: not a rascal, but *another* rascal.)

In 1884, Dietzgen moved to the United States for the third and last time, and became editor of the New York *Der Sozialist*, a position he retained until 1886, when he moved to Chicago. That year, the anarchist editors of the *Chicagoer Arbeiterzeitung* and the American-born anarchist, Albert Parsons, were arrested for the Haymarket bombing. In spite of the threats to his safety, and the ideological differences between socialists and anarchists, Dietzgen stepped in and continued publication of the paper despite having frequently been made fun of in the anarchist press for his socialist stance and rather old-fashioned prose style.

The Socialist Labor Party, of which Dietzgen was a member, tried to distance itself as far as possible from the Haymarket Martyrs and anarchism. The party leaders were outraged by the old tanner's support for the anarchists, but he would not be moved, declaring that he, too, was an anarchist. He wrote, "While anarchists may have many mad and brainless individualists in their ranks, the socialists have an abundance of cowards. For this reason I care about the one as much as the other. The majority in both camps are still in need of education and this will bring a reconciliation in time." Friedrich Engels, hearing about Dietzgen's sympathy for anarchism, was furious. Dietzgen survived the post-Haymarket anti-radical hysteria, but died of a heart attack two years later. He was buried alongside his new friends, the state-murdered Chicago anarchists.

His writings were well circulated in the early labor movement. Anton Pannekoek thought enough of them to write an introduction to the collection edited by Dietzgen's son, Eugene Dietzgen, *The Positive Outcome of Philosophy*.

Henrietta Roland-Holst of the German ultra-left was also a follower of Dietzgen. The IWW, the Socialist Party of Canada, the One Big Union and the Proletarian Party all lauded the Tanner. The Labour Colleges in Great Britain under Fred Casey taught Dietzgen's philosophy. Most Dietzgenists were supporters of the anti-Statist tendency of the workers' movement, of which the aforementioned groups were examples. Dietzgen's influence in politics was not to last. In part, it died with the demise of the libertarian socialist tendency in the aftermath of the Bolshevik Revolution. It was displaced by the mechanical "Dialectical Materialism" (Diamat) of Georgi Plechanov and Karl Kautsky. Stalin's version of Diamat became the state philosophy of the USSR. Now that the USSR is gone and Diamat with it, and new and global libertarian movement is on the rise, it is time to look once more at the writings of the "Proletarian Philosopher."

Cosmic Dialectics, The Libertarian Philosophy of Joseph Dietzgen

by Larry Gambone

Thinking About Thinking

Dietzgen began by asking the question, "What happens when we think?" He observed that the basic thinking process was essentially the same whether done by the greatest scientist or a common person. For "the simplest conception, or any idea for that matter, is of the same general nature as the most perfect understanding . . . Thought is work."[1]

By showing the common basis of thought, Dietzgen democratized science and philosophy. The belief that every person's opinion must be valued and that thinking must not be especially reserved for an intellectual elite puts him at variance with both academia and Marxist specialists in revolution. "The knowledge and study of this theory cannot be left to any particular guild . . . general thought is a public matter which everyone should be required to attend to himself."[2]

But what happens when we think? What is the innate process that underlies thought, whether thinking about plowing a field, contemplating the cosmos or just plain day-dreaming? Thought requires the formation of concepts about the world, a process which involves two differing aspects:

> By means of thought we become aware of all things in a twofold manner, outside in reality and inside in thought . . . Our brain does not assimilate the things themselves, but only their images. The imagined tree is only a general tree. The real tree is different from any other. And although I may have the picture of some special tree in my head, yet the real tree is still different from its conception as the specific is different from the general.[3]

One must not make the mistake of confusing one's mental pictures of the world with reality itself. The real, existing thing is not exactly like the generalization which is formed in the mind. "What abstract thing, being, existence, generality is there that is not manifold in its sense manifestations, and individually different from all other things? There are no two drops of water alike."[4]

Thought is a process of forming generalizations out of specific incidences or specific things. Thinking involves the specific and individual things of the world and our generalizations about them. Thought involves generalization.

> The common feature of all separate thought processes consists in their seeking the general character or unity which is common to all objects experienced in their manifold variety.[5]

But generalization isn't all we do when we think, nor is it without inherent problems. If we take our generalizations to an extreme, we can easily get lost in what are essentially our own mental constructions. We trap ourselves by thinking our productions are reality. This is what happens to people who get caught up in extreme religious or political cults. To bring ourselves back down to reality, it is necessary to never forget the individual and specific aspects of things.

> Mere generalization is one-sided and leads to fantastical dreams. By this method one can transform anything into everything. It is necessary to supplement generalization by specialization . . . the general must be conceived in its relation to its specific forms, and these forms in their universal interconnection.[6]

Contradiction Inherent in Thought

Thought is a process which involves a relationship between two opposing aspects: the aspect of generalization and the aspect of specialization. To think means to always be engaged in a contradictory process.

> For consciousness generalizes differences and differentiates generalities. Contradiction is innate in consciousness and its nature is so contradictory that it is at the same time a differentiating, a generalizing and an understanding nature. Consciousness . . . recognizes that all nature, all being, lives in contradictions, that everything is what it is only in co-operating with its opposite.[7]

As with generalization, here is a trap we must avoid. One can get so caught up in the contradictions confronting us that it becomes impossible to make decisions. However, it is possible to achieve some sort of balance or synthesis between opposite views and the contradictions can, at least in part, be overcome.

> Reason develops its understanding out of contradictions. It is in the nature of mind to

> perceive . . . the nature of things by their semblance, and their semblance by their nature . . . or in other words to compare the contrasts of the world with one and other, to harmonize them. [8]

The Limitations of Our Knowledge

It should be obvious by now, that this contradictory process of generalization or concept formation gives us only a limited understanding of the world. That ten people witnessing a traffic accident might have ten different versions of what happened is perfectly understandable. What we are doing is forming our concepts about the world through our thinking processes, resulting in a viewpoint which *approximates* reality, but is not reality itself. Hence, and this should be engraved on stone in letters two feet high, there is no perfect knowledge or truth.

> Our brain is supposed to solve the contradictions of nature. If it knows enough about itself to realize that it is not an exception from general nature . . . then it also knows that its clearness can differ but moderately from the general confusion . . . The contradictions are solved only by reasonable differentiation . . . extravagant differences are nothing but extravagant speculations . . . and it is a relic of untrained habits to differentiate in an absolute manner. [9]

"The rule [is] not to make exaggerated, but only graduated distinctions. Compared to the wealth of the Cosmos, the intellect is only a poor fellow." [10]

Given the difficulty of attaining a clear understanding of reality, it comes as no surprise that Dietzgen regarded truth in relative terms There could be no such thing as absolute truth. "A perfect understanding is possible only within limits."[11] While truth with a capital "T" is unattainable, this should not stop us from trying to get as near to the goal of absolute truth as possible. "The improvement in the method of thinking is like every other improvement, a limitless problem, the solution which must always remain unachieved. This, however, must in no way keep us from striving after it."[12]

The Importance of Error

For Dietzgen, no absolute separation existed between truth and error. All truths contain some amount of error, and all errors contain some amount of truth. "Truth and error differ only comparatively, in volume of degree . . . like all other opposites in the world . . . Everything, every sense perception, no matter how subjective is true, a certain part of truth."[13]

Aside from fanatics and dogmatists, it is not very difficult to admit a truth might contain some element of error, but what about the idea that truth can be found in error? This is not such an offbeat concept when you realize even the wildest dreams are based upon material ultimately taken from the real world, in the manner that the fantasy of the unicorn is constructed by mentally attaching a narwhal's horn upon the head of a horse. Error results from universalizing or absolutizing some aspect of limited applicability, or as in the case of the narwhal horn, placing something, which would otherwise be real and true, where it does not belong.

> Error . . . arises when the faculty of thought . . . inadvertently or short-sightedly and without previous experience concedes to certain phenomena a more general scope.[14]

In a nutshell, "unwarranted assumption is the nature of error."[15] Dogmatism is to be avoided.

> All distinctions are only quantitative, not absolute, only graduated, not irreconcilable . . . Instead of realizing the limited applicability of its rules by the existence of opposing practices, convention seeks to establish an absolute applicability of its rules by simply ignoring the cause of the opposition. This is a dogmatic procedure.[16]

One of the problems which Dietzgen does not deal with is error that disguises itself as truth. In this situation, arguments may be logical and contain obvious truths, yet often result in dangerous falsehoods. The false syllogism, such as contemporary far-right media's assertion "Terrorists oppose the US occupation of Iraq; socialists, too, oppose this occupation, therefore socialists are terrorists," is one example of this.

Thought Must Have an Object

Dietzgen made the observation that thought must have an object, i.e., one must think about some *thing*, even if this consists only of thinking about thought itself. Hence, there are no disembodied thoughts—thoughts without an object. These objects of thought are taken from the external world (and also from the psyche, a point not known by the pre-Freudian Dietzgen). Therefore, the world ultimately precedes human thought. In this manner, the Proletarian Philosopher declared himself to be a materialist, but he was not satisfied by the usual meaning of the term.

> We . . . must not be satisfied with simply following the example of the old materialist who reduced everything to ponderable atoms. Cosmic matter has not only gravity, but aroma, light and sound—and why not also intelligence? The conception of matter must be given a more comprehensive meaning. To it belongs all phenomena of reality.[17]

Idealism vs. Materialism

Dietzgen attributed the dispute between idealism and materialism to the absolutizing of the differences between the two concepts.

> The idealist regards reason alone as the source of all understanding, while the materialist looks upon the world of sense perceptions in the same way. Nothing is required for a solution of this contradiction but the comprehension of the relative interdependence of these two sources of understanding . . . But these distinctions belong to the one common genus which constitutes the distinction between the special and the general.[18]

Both idealists and materialists had an unreal conception of the world.

> The idealist overestimated the idea, the materialist matter, both were dreamers . . . both distinguished mind and matter in fantastic, unreal way. Neither of them raised themselves to the consciousness of unity and monism . . . of Nature which is not either material or mental, but one as well as the other.[19]

> The old materialists dealt in irreconcilable opposites just like the idealists.[20]

The world contains both mental and material, both are real and all that is real is what makes up the material world. Everything that has an effect upon the world is real, ie., material.

> We distinguish between the object of sense perception and its mental image. Nevertheless the intangible idea is also material and real. I perceive my idea of a desk just as plainly as the desk itself. True, if I choose to call only tangible things material, then ideas are not

> material . . . Mind is as real as the tangible table . . . While the idea of these things is different from the things themselves, yet it has that in common with them that it is as real as they are.[21]

The division between our ideas and the "real material reality" is not absolute. Consider the effect of the imagination. Our imaginary creations are both non-real (not existing) and yet have some reality since they are based ultimately upon the objectively existing world. These fantasies can also have a major impact upon us, think only of the insane ideas of Hitler or Stalin. According to Dietzgen, "there is only a moderate distinction of degree between purely imaginary things and so-called real things."[22]

Dietzgen also valued the imagination. Fantasy has certainly a positive power, and speculative intuition "very often precedes empirical and inductive understanding."[23]

Dietzgen's Critique of Bourgeois Materialism

Dietzgen attacked materialism as being itself a kind of idealism.

> Inasmuch as the materialist speaks ironically of formless matter and matterless forms, in the same breath with perishable forms of imperishable matter, it is plain that materialism is not any more informed than idealism as to the relation of content to form, of a phenomenon to the essential nature of its subject. Where do we find such eternal, imperishable, formless matter?[24]

Dietzgen had no patience for the argument that reduced ideas and the supposedly non-material to mere derivatives of "matter".

> Matter is to the old materialists the exalted subject, all other things subordinate prejudices . . . an

> antiquated, narrow thinking which has taken no notice of the work of German dialecticians. It must be understood that subjects are composed exclusively of predicates.[25]

There was a difference between the old materialism and the new which formed the philosophical basis of Social Democracy.

> We see the distinguishing mark between the mechanical materialists . . . and the Social Democratic materialists . . . in that the latter have extended the former's narrow conception of matter as consisting exclusively of the Tangible to all phenomena that occur in the world.[26]

It was wrong to separate mind and matter in an extreme fashion. The only way to come to an understanding of reality is to see the mental and physical in their unity. "Matter" is a mental construct, but "mind" cannot exist without the material world of objects and forces.

> Mind is material and things are mental. Mind and matter are real only in their interrelations.[27]

The word "matter" was not sacred for Dietzgen and he was not afraid to abandon it for a more inclusive term and thereby do away with the dualism of idealism vs. materialism.

> Solid and liquid, wood and metal are quite correctly summed up under the notion 'matter.' Why should we not be justified in summing up all things under the term 'empirical truth' or empirical phenomenon? . . . Through the common origins all antagonisms are reconciled and bridged over. Diversity is but a form: in their essence all things are alike . . . we find what is more and more being proved by natural science, that seemingly essential

> differences are but differences in degree . . . The cause effects and the effect causes. [28]

> And those who dislike this generalization of the word "matter" may instead, speak of "phenomena" . . . the name of the general species, to which everything belongs, the ponderable and the imponderable, body and soul. [29]

Nonetheless, he was willing to accept the name "materialist," but with a proviso:

> But now we Social Democrats accept the name [of materialists] with which our opponents think to abuse us, because we know that 'the stone which the builder refused is become the head corner stone.' We would equally be justified to call ourselves idealists, inasmuch as our system is based on the final results of philosophy, on the scientific investigation of ideas. [30]

In rejecting the materialism which reduced all phenomena to "matter," Dietzgen also rejected the theory of knowledge know as "reflection theory." This concept, developed by Lenin in *Materialism and Empireocriticism*, saw concepts and ideas as mere copies or reflections of the "material world," in the manner that a camera reproduces an image.

> Nothing more insipid has been said of truth and knowledge than . . . that truth is the conformity of our knowledge with its object. How can a picture "conform" to its model? Approximately it can . . . But to be altogether alike, quite the same as the original, what an abnormal idea! Thus we can only know Nature and her parts relatively, since even a part, though only a relation of Nature, possesses again the characteristics of the Absolute, the nature of the ALL- EXISTENCE which cannot be exhausted by knowledge. [31]

The Essential Unity of the World

Dietzgen called his philosophy monist, which refers to the view that all existence is ultimately unified.

> Consciousness is in itself consciousness of the infinite. Our settled conviction of the unity of the universe is an inborn logic. The unity of the world is the supreme and most universal category. A closer look . . . reveals the fact that it carries its opposite, the Infinite multiplicity.[32]

The unity of existence is innate in the human mind. "With our hands we grasp only the tangible, with our eyes only the visible, but with our conception we grasp the whole Nature, the Universe."[33]

The absolute separation of any aspect of existence from another, while not the ultimate truth about reality, was also a creation of the mind.

> Consciousness signifies the knowledge of being. It means having at least a faint inkling of the fact that being is the universal idea. Being is everything; it is the essence of everything . . . the human intellect knows of no absolute separation of any two things, although it is free to separate the universe into its parts for the purpose of understanding.[34]

Existence is the only absolute.

> Perfectly true, perfectly universal, is only the general existence, the Universe, the absolute quantity. But the real world is absolutely relative, absolutely perishable, an infinity of manifestations . . . All truths are simply parts of this world, partial truths . . . The general mark of truth is existence.[35]

Reality cannot be reduced to either ideas or matter, (both being human constructs) but the one "thing" it can be resolved into is the Universe or the Totality. Here, Dietzgen believed, was the only solid place to anchor a philosophy, for all finite concepts proved ultimately illusory. Upon this firm ground, Dietzgen was able to reconcile the classical problems of philosophy, such as free will vs. determinism, matter and force, cause and effect, and materialism vs. idealism. These opposites were not as opposed as people thought, or as he stated, "We do not conceive the forces as mere predicates of matter. Our conception of matter and force is, so to speak, democratic. One is of the same value as the other; everything individual is but the property . . . of the entire Nature."[36]

We assume the underlying unity of the world in our everyday actions, hence the Tanner's *a priori* is indeed a most basic assumption of our consciousness. We would not be able to function for any length of time without the associated concepts of the existence, coherence and oneness of the world. Science is based upon this essential idea and would be impossible without it. And if the world was dualistic, and there was another truly separate existence, we would not be able to know about it. Hence absolute separation is meaningless.

Cause and Effect

Dietzgen dealt rather extensively with the problem of cause and effect. Science searches for the reasons for events and it is considered an important discovery when a causal link is discovered. (We are told that germs cause disease.) The problem for both the metaphysician and the scientist is that we rarely find THE cause of something and our discoveries often give rise to more questions. (If germs cause disease, why are we not sick all the time, since we are continually surrounded by germs?)

> Thus things become mutual causes and mutual effects. The entire world of phenomena, of which

> thought is but a part, is an absolute circle, in which the beginning and end is everywhere and nowhere, in which everything is at the same time essence and semblance, cause and effect, general and concrete. Just as all Nature is in the last instance one sole general unity . . . so this same Nature . . . is the final cause of all things.[37]

Reason, and not sense perception, are the ultimate means through which we arrive at the notion of "cause."

> Causes are, in the last instance, not noticed and furnished by means of . . . the sense perceptions. They are supplied by the faculty of thought . . . not 'pure' products of the faculty of thought, but are produced by it in connection with sense perceptions . . . Causes are mental generalizations of perceptible changes . . . The speculative cause creates its effects. But in reality the effects are the material out of which the brain, or science, forms its causes. The cause concept is a product of reason . . . married to the world of sense perceptions.[38]

Thus Dietzgen once more combats arrogance, the sort one finds with the technocrat and his interminable "scientific plans," the dogmatic Marxist, or neo-liberal and his inflexible "economic laws." We should not glorify our discoveries, ideas or concepts, for these are all demarcations of reality we have made. Our knowledge is more than likely to be gray and fuzzy rather than sharply outlined in black and white. Not that our mental toil results in complete untruth or everything is subjective fantasy, but our constructs are merely an *approximation* of reality. As the millions of victims of twentieth-century arrogance can attest, our knowledge is always limited, partial knowledge, and to think otherwise is to fall into a deep and dangerous error.

The Problem of Language

Dietzgen realized that many problems of philosophy arose with the inadequate use of language. In this manner, he foreshadowed Wittgenstein and the analytic philosophers.

> The inertia which has prevented the one-sided idealists on the one hand and the one-sided materialists on the other from coming to a peaceful understanding may be traced to one of those slips of the tongue. We lack the right terms for designating the relationship between spiritual phenomena . . . and the tangible . . . things on the other.[39]

He did not take words as reality, as do so many intellectuals, but regarded them as symbols. "Words are names, which do not, and cannot, have anyother function than that of symbolic illustration."[40]

Science vs. Scientism

Like virtually all nineteenth-century thinkers, Dietzgen considered his works to be scientific. By this time, (the 1870s) the term "science" began to change meaning. Previously, any organized body of knowledge was considered a science and there was nothing smacking of pretentiousness or scientism in speaking about the "science of cookery" or "scientific socialism." With the rise of Positivism and materialism came a new and more restricted use of the word. The term "science" was now reduced to those areas of inquiry which applied the methodology of the natural sciences. Positivism engaged in a search for the immutable laws of nature which supposedly existed independently of the observer. Any other approach was deemed unscientific or pseudo-science and condemned in language similar to that used by sixteenth-century heresy-hunters. Science had become a new absolutism and a new superstition. This was too much for the Tanner to stomach.

> There are among us a good many people who, instead of regarding science as a handmaid to civilization, idolize and worship it . . . They are like the barbarians who turned the natural and social law into a divinity . . . It is incumbent upon social democracy to destroy both religious and scientific superstition.[41]

He reproached scientists and academics for their elitism and considered them as idealistic (in the philosophical sense) as the materialists whose philosophical offspring they undoubtedly were.

> Having materialized everything spiritual, there remained nothing for the professors but to spiritualize their own profession, science. They assume academic knowledge to be of a different type than say, the knowledge of the peasant, the dyer or the smith. Scientific agriculture is, however, only insofar ahead of usual farming that its rules or knowledge of the so-called natural laws are generalizations of a more comprehensive kind. They but differ from each other in degree and not in essence . . . we want to overcome the claims of the aristocracy of intellect.[42]

Natural science had not yet abandoned the old mechanical materialism. "Modern science is even today still animated by the bias of the materialists of the 18th Century."[43]

The ultimate science was philosophy.

Positive science can give us knowledge of many aspects of the world, but it is left to another form of thinking (or science) to understand the world. Natural science is subordinate in one sense to philosophy—the science which investigates those basic questions that natural scientists usually take for granted—questions such as, "What is thought?", "What is truth?" and "Why Existence when there could be nothing?" Positivist science refuses to even allow such questions to be asked, a rather unscientific and illogical approach to say the least.

> Natural science in its narrower sense cannot give us the monistic conception of the world . . . [this] is investigated by a separate science some call Logic, or Epistemology or Dialectics. [44]

Dietzgen's Individualism

Rooted in the concept that all thought is in essence similar, Dietzgen's philosophy is from the beginning democratic and egalitarian. One person may know more than another, but the differences between individuals are only quantitative, not qualitative. To be human is to have the capacity for reason. Such a viewpoint has a high regard for the individual, since each person's opinion, and therefore each person, is seen as having intrinsic value.

An essential concept of individuality also exists within his philosophy, shown by his belief that each drop of water differs from every other. And if water drops are individuals, consider the individuality of that complex creature, Homo sapiens, or as he stated,"humanity is an idea, while man is always some special person." [45]

Dietzgen's Concept of History

Dietzgen's concept of history is related to his evaluation of the individual. "It is only the consciousness of individual freedom which creates sufficient unconcern for the rules made by others to permit a brave advance, which emancipates us from striving for an illusory absolute ideal, for some "best world." [46]

This unconcern for the rules made by others allowed him to break with the SLP and go to the aid of the beleaguered anarchists. At a time when a highly determinist view of history virtually expunged the factor of human will, the

Tanner noted that "humanity revolutionizes its highest standards, in short, it makes history."[47] His holistic view of man, history, and nature protected him from falling into both the utopian trap and its opposite, the sort of despair we see so much of today. Nor did he have a blind belief in progress like so many of his contemporaries.

> Progress picks up the child and then pours the water out of the bathtub . . . The present wealth of civilization is due only to the economic administration of the acquirements of the past. Evolution is as much conservative as it is revolutionary, and it finds as much wrong as right in every law.[48]

Dietzgen, like most Marxists, thought that class society was a necessary stage in human history.

> I am even inclined to admit that the task of developing our labor power to that degree of prodigious fertility which we see today, has necessitated a privileged governing class as well as the exploitation of the masses. I am ready to acquiesce patiently in the misery of the past, and bear it no grudge or malice.[49]

Social evolution is not nihilistic, no clean-slate wiping away of the past and as much is retained as is rejected. Both the radical and the conservative are necessary. Nor is there a need to have someone to blame for the world's ills, history just IS and we are all part of it.

> At the same time we are thus reconciled with the world as it really is, because we no longer regard it as the unsuccessful realization of that which cannot but be. The world is always right. Whatever exists, is right and is not fated to be otherwise until it changes. Wherever there is existence, which is power, there is also right without further condition, because it is right

> in a formative stage. Weakness has no other right than striving for supremacy . . . forcing a recognition of its long denied needs.[50]

Unlike some anarchists who think it possible to completely abolish power, Dietzgen recognized that existence is power. The "weak" he refers to are undoubtedly the laboring classes, who in their struggle for recognition of their needs, overcome their weakness. That "the world is always right" seems appalling in an era which has seen the likes of Pol Pot and Hitler. However, this restatement of Hegel's oft quoted and always misunderstood "Real is Rational" is not a whitewash of the crimes of history. It merely states that history is a process in which events have causes—in the limited sense of cause and effect that Dietzgen uses. Hitler, for example, did not fall from the sky, nor were the German people seized by temporary madness; his rise to power was caused the racism and authoritarianism of European society, the punitive Versailles Treaty, the destruction of the middle class, their fear of social revolution etc.

Dietzgen and the Spiritual

We have seen in Dietzgen's philosophy that human knowledge is limited and that the only Absolute which exists is the Totality of Existence or the Universe. (By Universe, he did not mean what astronomers mean by it, rather he meant Existence—all that has ever happened, all that is happening now, all that will happen). He observed that if the anthropomorphism, superstition and hocus pocus were stripped away from religion what was left was the Absolute. God is another word for the Absolute or the Totality of Existence,

> the all perfect Being, with the conception of God, with the Substance of Spinoza, with the "thing in itself" of Kant, and with the Absolute of Hegel, has its good reason in the fact that the sober conception of the

> Universe as the All-One with nothing above or outside or alongside of it, is the first postulate of a skilled and consistent mode of thinking.[51]

Religion had both positive and negative aspects. "History shows us not only the negative and ridiculous side of the religions, customs, institutions and ideas of the past, but also their positive, reasonable and necessary side . . . when religion was a more serious affair, it was also less dualistic."[52]

> The devil was but a tool, the earthly life but a transitional term of probation for the eternal life. There was a centre of gravity and system. In comparison with modern half-heartedness . . . religion did encompass the whole in a monistic manner.[53]

While cruelty, superstition and control of the lower classes are major elements of religion it could not be written off as just this. Like everything else, religion has a rational core. He did not blush at being called an atheist, but religion didn't terrify him.

> If he is an atheist who denies that perfection can be found in an individual, then I am an atheist. And if he is a believer in God who has the faith in the "most perfect being" with which not alone theologists, but also Cartesius and Spinoza have occupied themselves, then I am one of the true children of God.[54]

According to Dietzgen, the problem with religion was that it personified God as symbol such as the Father or the Divine King, and the symbol came to be taken for the reality. Thus, we have the childish view of God as an old man on a cloud writing down our sins in a great book. The Absolute is far beyond anything so earth-bound and anthropomorphic as personification, or as Dietzgen stated, "the infinite, eternal, is not personal, but objective."[55]

Orthodox religion had become overly transcendental and had forgotten immanence—the Absolute had been removed from the world and this was wrong.

> The relative and the absolute do not lie so far apart as it is painted to man by that uncultivated sense of Infinity called Religion . . . The Absolute and the Relative are not separated transcendentally, they are connected with each other so that the Unlimited is made up of an infinite number of finite limitations and each limited phenomenon possesses the nature of the Infinite. [56]

One final quote shows attitudes reminiscent of the Sermon On The Mount: "Never be harsh in your judgments of others . . . In order to act courteously, you must think courteously. Virtue and faults are combined. Even the rascal is a good fellow and the just sins seven times a day." [57]

Dietzgen's Politics

While living in Germany, Dietzgen was a member of the Social Democratic Party. This did not mean he was a State Socialist. What he proposed was a system of co-operative production and not State ownership: humanity's "savior can only be found in cooperative, brotherly work." [58]

A cooperative society was one without class division. "Only from the abolition of class rule, from the transformation of the selfish capitalistic organizations into co-operative instruments of production will issue the true brotherhood of man." [59]

How was the co-operative commonwealth to come about? Certainly not through the manipulations of a gang of academic know-it-alls or New Bosses. It was necessary to

> emancipate the working class through the workers themselves . . . a more equitable and popular distribution of economic goods can be realized by a

> democracy only [not] the rule of a clique under the pretense of intellectual superiority.[60]

Social change would not come about through missionary work, nor utopian schemes. Salvation comes not from religious, political and social enlightenment, but grows organically out of the development of social economy. (Dietzgen, like all the Marxists of his day, was overly optimistic about the demise of capitalism.)

> We don't look for salvation in subjective schemes, but we see it growing as a sort of organic product out of the inevitable course of actual development. All we do is facilitate its birth. . . . which emancipates us from striving for an illusory absolute ideal, for some "best world"[61]

And also:

> We too demand the restoration of our human rights . . . this . . . is no idle speculation, but is the natural outcome of present material wants . . . [the cooperative economy is] . . . quite in keeping with the nature of the present system: it must come: its materials are being produced and multiplied daily. The capitalists are the real silk-worms . . . The premature question about the future, When, Where, and How need not trouble us, it is indeed an idle 'philosophic' speculation.[62]

Dietzgen foreshadowed the IWW's idea of "New in the shell of the old": "The society we are striving for differs from the present but by modifications. The society of the future is contained in the present society as the young bird is in the egg."[63]

Positivism with its so-called Eternal Laws was rejected in politics as well as philosophy. Nor must activists do more than educate in the broadest sense. They are not military commanders:

> Social Democracy does not seek to establish eternal laws, permanent institutions or unchangeable forms; it seeks the salvation of mankind. The indispensable means . . . is mental enlightenment.[64]

Dietzgen's philosophy, founded on tolerance, could only demand a political practice that was tolerant and allowed a broad range of opinions to exist: "We must in practice be tolerant in the extreme and surely no Social Democrat would ever think of putting any Party member into a straight jacket of uniformity."[65]

Economics

There is little in English on Dietzgen's economic ideas. That which does exist is interesting in the way it foreshadows later developments. Unlike many socialists of his day, he saw that a well paid work force was necessary for economic development, whether capitalist or social democratic.

> The prime necessity to an advance in civilization is freedom of the people to participate in consumption . . . wealth, once the stimulator of progress, is now turning into a factor of historical stagnation . . . on the whole it must be admitted that the growth of production is kept in check by the question of consumption.[66]

But the capitalist was too concerned with immediate profit to increase wages.

> Business is at a standstill, and there is no demand for goods. The only way out of this calamity is participation of the masses in consumption; the wages must be increased and labor time reduced. But the well-fed capitalist . . . is too narrow minded to pay the producer of his wealth, the worker, well . . . Not only social democracy, but the national economics demand a larger consumption, a wider market for its products.[67]

Endnotes

1 Joseph Dietzgen, *The Nature of Human Brain Work* (Oakland: PM Press, 2010), 18.

2 Ibid., 6.

3 Ibid., 20.

4 Ibid., 44.

5 Ibid., 27.

6 Joseph Dietzgen, *The Positive Outcome of Philosophy*, trans. Ernest Untermann (Chicago: Charles H. Kerr, 1906), 357.

7 Ibid., 33.

8 Ibid., 88.

9 Ibid., 350.

10 Ibid., 430.

11 Dietzgen, *The Nature of Human Brain Work*, 47.

12 Joseph Dietzgen, *The Positive Outcome of Philosophy*, (Chicago: Kerr, 1906), 265.

13 Dietzgen, *The Nature of Human Brain Work*, 43.

14 Ibid., 47.

15 Ibid., 48.

16 Ibid., 83

17 Joseph Dietzgen, *Some of the Philosophical Essays*, trans. M. Beer and Th. Rothstein (Chicago: Charles H. Kerr, 1906), 221.

18 op cit., 69.

19 Dietzgen, *Some of the Philosophical Essays*, 294.

20 Ibid., 298.

21 Dietzgen, *The Nature of Human Brain Work*, 19.

22 Dietzgen, *The Positive Outcome of Philosophy*, 367.

23 Ibid., 9.

24 Dietzgen, *The Nature of Human Brain Work*, 34.

25 Dietzgen, *Some of the Philosophical Essays*, 295.

26 Ibid., 298.

27 Dietzgen, *The Nature of Human Brain Work*, 21.

28 Dietzgen, *Some of the Philosophical Essays*, 5.

29 Ibid., 218.

30 Ibid.
31 Ibid., 140.
32 Dietzgen, *The Positive Outcome of Philosophy*, 410.
33 Ibid., 45.
34 Ibid., 361.
35 Dietzgen, *The Nature of Human Brain Work*, 42.
36 Dietzgen, *Some of the Philosophical Essays*, 301.
37 Dietzgen, *The Nature of Human Brain Work*, 58.
38 Dietzgen, *The Positive Outcome of Philosophy*, 438.
39 Ibid., 361.
40 Dietzgen, *Some of the Philosophical Essays*, 103.
41 Ibid., 103.
42 Ibid., 128.
43 Ibid., 299.
44 Ibid., 220.
45 Dietzgen, *The Nature of Human Brain Work*, 107.
46 Ibid., 96.
47 Dietzgen, *Some of the Philosophical Essays*, 113.
48 Dietzgen, *The Nature of Human Brain Work*, 95.
49 Dietzgen, *Some of the Philosophical Essays*, 97.
50 Ibid., 109.
51 Ibid., 274.
52 Dietzgen, *The Nature of Human Brain Work*, 96.
53 Dietzgen, *Some of the Philosophical Essays*, 148.
54 Dietzgen, *The Positive Outcome of Philosophy*, 244.
55 Ibid., 437.
56 Dietzgen, *Some of the Philosophical Essays*, 288–289.
57 *Industrial Worker*, April 17, 1937.
58 Dietzgen, *Some of the Philosophical Essays*,108.
59 Ibid., 160.
60 Ibid., 127–131.
61 Dietzgen, *Some of the Philosophical Essays*, 179.
62 Ibid., 191–2.
63 From the *Volkstaadt*, as quoted in *Industrial Worker*, April 17, 1937.
64 Dietzgen, *Some of the Philosophical Essays*, 225.

65 Ibid.

66 Dietzgen, *Some of the Philosophical Essays*, 98–99.

67 Ibid., 178.

A Dietzgen Bibliography

Books

Casey, Fred. *Dietzgen's Logic*. Manchester: Express Co-op, 1928.

Casey, Fred. *Thinking*. Chicago: Charles H. Kerr, 1926.

Dietzgen, Eugene. *Dietzgen Brevier*. Munich, 1915.

Dietzgen, Josef. *Erkenntnis und Wahrheit. Des Arbeiter-philosophen universelle Denkweise und naturmonistische Anschauung über Lebenskunst, Ökonomie, Philosophie, Religion und Sozialismus. Gesammelt und herausgegeben von Eugen Dietzgen*. Stuttgart: Dietz, 1908.

Dietzgen, Joseph. *The Positive Outcome of Philosophy*. Translated by Ernest Untermann. Chicago: Charles H. Kerr, 1906.

Dietzgen, Josef. *Sämtliche Schriften*. Hrsg. v. Eugen Dietzgen. Stuttgart: Verlag der Dietzgenschen Philosophie, 1911.

Dietzgen, Joseph. *Some of the Philosophical Essays*. Translated by M. Beer and Th. Rothstein. Chicago: Charles H. Kerr, 1906.

Dietzgen, Joseph. *The Nature of Human Brain Work*. Translated by Ernest Untermann. Vancouver: Red Lion Press, 1984.

Hepner, Adolf. *Josef Dietzgens Philosophische Lehren Mit einem Porträt von Josef Dietzgen*. Stuttgart: Dietz, 1916.

Roland-Hoslt, Henreitta. *Joseph Dietzgens Philosophie.* Munich, 1910.

Sesic, Bogdan. *Dialectical Materialism of Joseph Dietzgen.* 1957.

Untermann, Ernest. *Die logische Mangel den engergen Marxismus, Georg Plechanove et alii gegen Josef Dietzgen.* Munich, 1910.

Articles

Buick, Adam. "Joseph Dietzgen." *Radical Encyclopedia of the Social Sciences* (1931) London.

Burns, Tony. "Joseph Dietzgen and the History of Marxism." *Science & Society* 66, no. 2 (2002): 202–227.

Casey, Fred. "Joseph Dietzgen." *The Plebs* (December 1928).

Easton, Lloyd, "Empiricism and Ethics in Dietzgen." *History of Ideas* 19, no. 1.

Doblin, A.A. "The Proletarian Philosophy of Joseph Dietzgen." *Radical Review* (January 1919).

Emmett, Dorothy. "Joseph Dietzgen, the Philosopher of Proletarian Logic." *Journal of Adult Education* (October 1928).

Hitch, Marcus. "Dietzgenism." *International Socialist Review* (November 1907).

Hogben, Lancelot. "The Wisdom of Joseph Dietzgen." *The Plebs* (May 1919).

Industrial Worker, "Dietzgen Recalled." (April 17, 1937).

Keracher, John. "Joseph Dietzgen." *The Proletarian.* December 1928.

Mehring, Franz. "Philosophy and Philosophizing." *Marxist Quarterly* (April–June 1937): 293–297.

Review Marxiste. "Joseph Dietzgen." (April 1929).

Swanson, Manley T. "Joseph Dietzgen and His Work." *The Proletarian* (January 1928).

Untermann, Ernest. "A Pioneer of Proletarian Science." *International Socialist Review* (April 1906).

Books that mention Dietzgen at some length

Aldred, Guy. *Pioneers of Anti-parliamentarianism*. Glasgow: Strickland Press, 1940.

Bricaner, Serge. *Pannekoek and the Workers' Councils*. St Louis: Telos Press, 1978.

Campbell, J. Peter. *Canadian Marxists and the Search for a Third Way*. Montreal: McGill-Queen's University Press, 1999.

Craik, W.W. *The Central Labour College*. London: Lawrence and Wishart, 1964.

Jackson, T. A. *Dialectics, the Logic of Marxism, and Its Critics, an Essay in Exploration*. New York: International Publishers, 1936.

Lenin, Vladimir. *Materialism and Empiriocriticism*. Moscow: Progress Publishers, 1960.

Macintyre, Stuart. *A Proletarian Science: Marxism in Britain 1917–1933*. Cambridge: Cambridge University Press, 1980.

Nizan, Paul. *The Watchdogs: Philosophers and the Established Order*. Translated by Paul Fittingoff. New York: Monthly Review Press, 1972.